Laser Cutting for Fashion and Textiles

Laura Berens Baker

Laser Cutting for Fashion and Textiles

Laura Berens Baker

Laurence King Publishing

Contents

Downloadable associated material, including templates of the pattern pieces, is available from the Laurence King website at www.laurenceking.com

Introduction: laser cutting as craft

Laser cutting is a very versatile digital technology that can be used to cut and decorate a wide range of materials, including textiles, acrylics and wood, with intricate designs and patterns.

Laser cutting does not preclude craftsmanship; it can, in fact, embrace and enhance it, using science, design and craft hand in hand. Many of the projects in this book take inspiration from traditional craft techniques and show how laser cutting can be used to evoke and reflect traditional finishes while also developing new ones. The surface-embellishment capabilities of the laser-cutting machine can be used to upcycle all manner of different fabrics, and can also be used to engineer and cut complete garments from a single piece of cloth.

Pioneered as a subtractive manufacturing technology, laser cutting was initially used in the 1960s and '70s for industrial applications. It is now used in the production of many products including furniture, models, jewellery and toys. As the technology has become more accessible, fashion and accessory designers, as well as textile designers, have incorporated laser cutting into their work. It can be used on a range of fabrics such as felt, linen, cotton and silk.

With the machinery now available in small-scale bureaux, and the software to drive those machines more widely used, it is possible for the consumer with just a little technical knowledge to design and make their own garments and accessories using laser cutting.

Isabella Joly's degree-show collection of menswear shirting and jacket fabrics was based on mapped landscapes. Joly was influenced by the imagery from Scandinavian naval maps and the tactility of Braille maps. The collection explored the woven quality of denim through laser etching and made use of techniques such as bonding and the coating of different fabrics in order to interpret the look or feel of denim.

The projects

This book will introduce you to the key tools, equipment and materials for using laser cutting for fashion, accessory and textile design. Beginning with simpler designs and products, the book advances through to more complex, creative constructions.

You can take your inspiration from many different sources. Much of the inspiration in this book comes from existing textile structures, with many of the patterns engineered into placement patterns or block or half-drop repeats:

* engineered trompe-l'oeil pebble shapes for the vest;
* a chevron effect for the belt;
* netting for the iPad case;
* broderie anglaise lace for the skirt;
* monogramming for the shopper;
* a basketweave pattern for the clutch bag;
* knitting machine punch cards for the jumper dress;
* honeycomb geometric structures for the jacket;
* a cable-knit pattern for the jumper top;
* wax-print designs for the long-sleeved dress.

Textile surface patterning also acts as inspiration for other projects:

* devoré-style embossing for the vest;
* trompe-l'oeil antique jewellery for one of the pendants;
* wood-veneer geometric shapes inspired by marquetry for the shawl and bangles.

Everyday objects have acted as inspiration for some of the designs, too – for example, an envelope is used as the basis for the design of the clutch bag, and a paper bag for the

Fiona Blakeman was inspired by the work of Jean Arp and of Helmut Newton – and by fishnet. In this collection she followed the natural imperfections and holes in her leather substrate to create the laser-cut pattern of each leather skin.

Laser cutting can achieve many different effects when used on a variety of fabrics:

etched faux suede

shopper. You can also take patterns from existing garments. The cable-knit top and the sweater-style dress were inspired by existing sweaters, while the jacket was inspired by a floor-length coat. While the projects in this book are inspired largely by the surface patterning produced in the production of various textiles, laser cutting offers such versatility that you can take your inspiration from just about anywhere.

Elements left over from one design can also be recycled and used in another: the shapes that drop out when the net design is cut for the iPad cover, for example, can be reused to create a relief version of the design if bonded on to a plain template. Pieces cut for the veneer of the bangles can be reused for the pendants.

The projects use a variety of materials, including ponyskin, suede and faux suede, jersey, cotton, silk, boiled wool, polyester, leather, acrylic and wood, while decorative and mark-making techniques include engraving, flocking, foiling and vinyl cutting. Polyesters, silks, wool felt, paper, leathers, fleece and acetate all work well for laser cutting, because the cutter will fuse the edges, preventing any fraying. Denim, fleece, suede, and reflective and coated fabrics are good choices for etching.

Other materials you can use include acrylonitrile butadiene styrene (ABS), styrene, polypropylene and other plastics, block foam, cork, paper and card, rubber and other fabrics including felt, denim, linen, nylon, neoprene and chiffon.

It is important to experiment with materials. You will need to get the technician who is realizing your work to test your materials before you go ahead with cutting. They will be able to find the best setting for your particular fabric. At this stage you can also see how your design works and edit the settings, detail in the file or scale of design accordingly. Etching can be costly, as can cutting right through an acrylic.

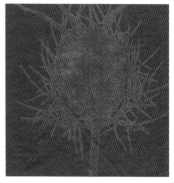

etched felt

laser-cut industrial felt

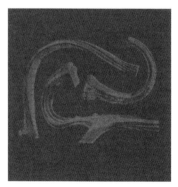

etched wool flannel

laser-cut and bonded
double-sided felt

How to use this book

A laser-cutting machine works by directing a beam of concentrated light that is capable of cutting through different materials. Most of the laser cutters found in art colleges are CO_2 machines with a power output of 85W. These cut by melting, burning or vaporizing a material. They are capable of cutting through most materials apart from metals and other hard materials (including glass, ceramics and hard woods such as thick plywood) although they are able to engrave them. PVC should be avoided, too, as it will produce acid smoke in the cutter.

The instructions for where and how to cut are given to the machine in the form of a CAD file created using vector-based software. Software used includes AutoCAD® by Autodesk, SOLIDWORKS by Dassault Systèmes, Rhinoceros® (Rhino) by Robert McNeel & Associates, Adobe Illustrator and SketchUp.

The 14 tutorials in this book will enable you to create CAD files in Adobe Illustrator to direct the laser-cutting machine to make the pieces for a range of different garments and accessories. You can use the laser cutter to cut out the pattern pieces and also decorate the material either by cutting, scoring or engraving (etching). The latter two processes are where the laser cuts into, but not completely through, the material; engraving is deeper than scoring.

Most students take files to the machine engineer or bureau and the technician does the cutting. The technician will produce a sample for approval and then produce the final job. You must brief the technician when you supply the files so that they understand your key (different coloured lines for different kinds of cut). The technician will have experience of working on a range of substrates. They will work out the correct setting for your files and quote you a price for the job.

The downloadable associated material for this book available at www.laurenceking.com contains all the components you need to make each of the projects, including templates of the pattern pieces and photos and illustrations, which you can trace to use as a basis for the different surface embellishments.

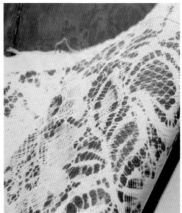

Bethan Wood's 'link' is a jewellery range made from a single sheet of birch ply, which focuses on producing minimal material wastage. The range is made from a series of repeated octagons, which decrease in size, allowing for all subsequent links to be cut from the space inside the largest. The links can form a variety of accessories from long chains to rings. In addition, 'link' celebrates the marks left by the process, incorporating the discolouration caused by laser cutting.

Elisa Strozyk creates 'wooden textiles' by laser cutting pieces of wood and then attaching them to a textile base. The result seems familiar but feels strange, challenging our expectations of the material. This dress is by Léa Peckre.

Kate Goldsworthy is interested in pioneering design solutions for the recycling ('upcycling') and reuse of polyesters. The end products are completely recyclable. In this example, she has added surface patterning and composite structure to a synthetic textile on a flat-bed system in a single laser-finishing process.

Setting up your Illustrator files

Note

There is almost always more than one way to achieve the same thing in Illustrator; by necessity, each tutorial in this book shows a single method.

Size

Always draw at full-scale.

It can help if you draw a bounding box for your artwork the same size as your material. Try to leave at least a 3-mm (1/8-inch) gap between the edge of the artwork and the bounding box.

You will need to check the bed size of the laser cutter to ensure it is large enough for your material. The iPad and pendants in this book could be cut on a smaller machine, for example, but the dresses will need a larger machine. Laser-bed dimensions vary, with sizes including 1200 x 700 mm (47 x 28 inches), 1200 x 900 mm (47 x 35 inches), 1450 x 990 mm (57 x 39 inches) and 2400 x 1200 mm (94 x 47 inches). Some studios may only have a machine with a smaller bed than these, while others will have a range of sizes and will use the most appropriate for your design.

Line colour

Most studios will set up their laser-cutting machines to recognize specific colours for different types of cut; an external cut for the outside of the pattern piece, an internal cut for shapes cut within, and a different colour for etched lines where you do not want the machine to cut right through your material. In this book the files are set up using RGB with the following selections:

External cut: magenta (R:255, G:0 and B:255)
Internal cut: green (R:0, G:255 and B:0)
Laser etch: blue (R:0, G:0 and B:255)

Line width

Set up your files with lines saved at a hairline thickness. The laser cutter will recognize fine lines and it will ensure that not too much material is cut away, allowing you to create a design with fine detail.

In this book the magenta, green and blue lines are changed to a stroke weight of 0.05 pt only at the end of the drawing process to allow you to see more clearly while working. Black lines are not used to direct the laser, so their width does not matter.

Other considerations

Importing images into Illustrator

You can use the Image Trace function within Illustrator to change an imported image into vectors to incorporate within your drawing. Select the image using the Selection tool and then choose Object > Image Trace.

You can also embed an image within your drawing. Select the image using the Selection tool, and click the Embed button from the Linked File control panel. Check that the Embedded Link icon appears next to the image in the Links panel (Window > Links).

Illustrator functions incompatible with laser cutting

You cannot use the Clipping Mask function or the Live Paint function within Illustrator for laser cutting. Release both: View > Outline and then use Object > Clipping Mask > Release or Object > Live Paint > Release. You will then need to trace or redraw the object or pattern.

Removing stray lines and vector points

Check that your drawing does not include any overlapping strokes; the laser cutter will repeatedly cut over any duplicated lines, which will ruin the material and damage the laser cutter. Identify any darker strokes, select them using the Direct Selection tool and then delete (Edit > Cut) until a single line remains.

Check that there are no outlines that you do not want cut or engraved. View > Outline and then erase any that you do not want using the Erase tool from the Tools panel.

You also need to clear all the guides and any stray vector points. Select Select > Object > Stray Points and View > Guides > Clear Guides.Ensure vector paths are simple and continuous, and that all shapes are closed.

Reduce the number of vector points if possible to help speed up the laser-cutting process. Select the object or path you wish to adjust and choose Object > Path > Simplify. Adjust the sliders until you are happy with the balance between the number of anchor points and the appearance of the drawing.

Join and close any open paths and shapes by selecting the open endpoints with the Direct Selection tool and then selecting Object > Path > Join.

If you have any objects nested within each other, check that there is a 2-mm ($\frac{1}{12}$-inch) gap between them.

Sending the files to the laser cutter

The technician printing your work will usually check the file first, work out what needs to be tested and then provide a cost, usually in terms of time. Files may be returned for adjustment. Testing and sampling may be charged in addition to the final cost, and any mistakes in the drawing are always the responsibility of the designer.

Once testing is complete and potential problems are resolved, the technician will choose the most suitable machine for the design and the material being cut.

Depending on the material, a peel-away protective backing may be used to protect the surface from heat and burn marks.

Making instructions

Sewing or assembly instructions are given for each tutorial, but you will need to select the most appropriate method of completing your project according to the materials you have used.

Vest / allover pebble design

This tutorial demonstrates how to:

* engineer a found pattern to make a surface design to apply to your substrate;

* create a pattern for a simple, symmetrical vest;

* apply your surface design to your garment using laser-cut vinyl or fabric shapes.

The vest is made here in a white cotton piqué, and the black design is vinyl cut. The all-white design uses the same file, and cut-outs of the same fabric are applied using adhesive. You could use the files produced in this tutorial to make the vest in any material and use a variety of heat-transfer vinyls, foils or flocks for the appliqué detail.

Step 1

For this project you can use the file provided on the website for your pattern, pebble_pattern.ai and move straight to Step 5, or create your own.

Create a new document with an artboard size of 2000 mm (78.74 in) wide and 2000 mm (78.74 in) high, and name it pebble_pattern. In Advanced Options change the Colour Mode to RGB and click OK. **File > New**

Place your original photograph. **File > Place**

Step 2

Next, you need to identify and copy individual pebbles from within the design on the photograph to re-form into your own design. Start by selecting the area of the pattern that you wish to trace with the Selection tool. Then select the Image Trace button at the top of the document window.

Step 2 (continued)

Choose Expand at the top of the document window to convert the tracing into paths.

Double-click the object with the Selection tool to isolate the individual pebbles.

Then, holding the Shift key down, click on the pebbles you wish to use for your new pattern.

To copy the pebbles select **Edit > Copy.**

Now click the arrow (Back one level) at the top left of the screen and then click the arrow again to Exit Isolation Mode.

Step 2 (continued)

Paste the copied pebbles to the side of the original in the open document. **Edit > Paste**

Step 3

Having copied the pebbles, you can now start to rearrange them. Start by creating a square around which to arrange your design. **View > Outline**

Select the Rectangle tool from the Tools panel and, holding down the Shift key, draw a square next to your pebbles. Change both the W value and the H value in the Control panel to 760 mm (29.92 in).

With the square still selected, select a fill of None in the Tools panel.

Step 3 (continued)

Now select the rectangle and the pebble shapes with the Selection tool.

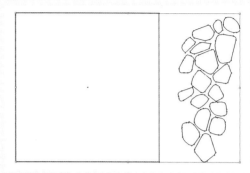

To help arrange the pebbles around the outline of the square, first identify the centre of each pebble by selecting **Window > Attributes**. In the Attributes panel, click the panel menu icon and select Show Centre.

To ensure the centre of each pebble is arranged around the outline of the square, choose **View > Smart Guides** and **View > Snap to Point**.

Selecting and dragging each pebble individually, arrange them along one side of the square, allowing each one to snap to the outline.

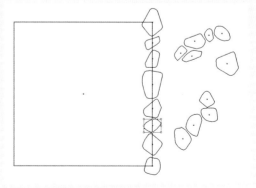

Holding down the Shift key, select each pebble with the Selection tool. Then, clicking on the path around one of the pebbles, hold down the Alt key and drag to create a copy, moving it to the other side of the square.

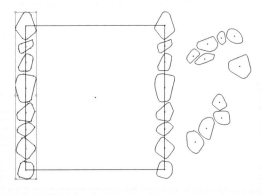

Repeat along the lower side of the square, this time copying the line and moving it to the top.

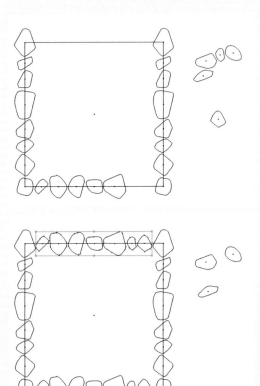

Now fill the square with pebbles to complete the pattern. You can duplicate pebbles by selecting the outline path of the pebble with the Selection tool, then holding down the Alt key and dragging to create a copy.

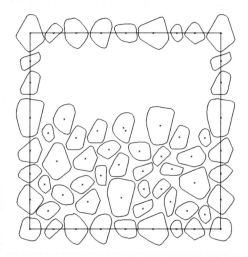

If you need to change the angle of a pebble to make it fit, you can hold down the Control key and click the mouse to bring up a menu; select **Transform > Rotate**, then adjust the angle in the dialogue box. Alternatively, you can select the pebble, use the mouse to hover outside one corner of it and then use the arrows that will appear to rotate the pebble.

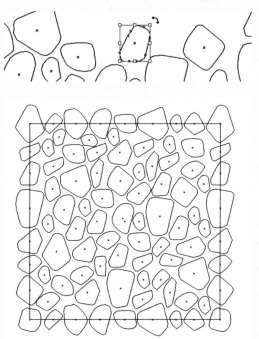

Step 4

To create a red outline around the pebbles, first select the outline of the square only.

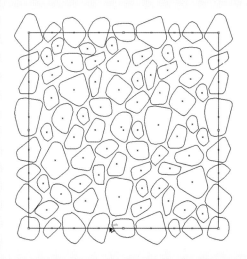

Hold down the Control key and click the mouse to bring up a menu; select Arrange and then Send to Back. Then select **View > Preview**.

Now select the top left-hand pebble. Choose **Select > Same > Fill Colour**.

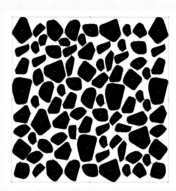

In the Appearance panel, choose a stroke of red (R:255, G:0 and B:0). Select a fill of None.

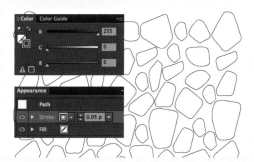

Step 4 (continued)

Finally, to create a swatch for this pattern, choose **Select > All** and then drag the pattern into your Swatches panel.

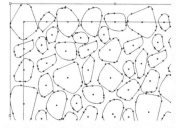
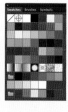

Click the panel menu icon in the Swatches panel and select Save Swatch Library as AI ... and save as vest_pattern_swatches.ai.

Now choose **File > Save As** and save your document as pebble_pattern.ai.

Step 5

Next, you need to draw your vest shape before filling it with your pebble pattern.

Start by creating a new document with an artboard size of 2000 mm (78.74 in) wide and 2000 mm (78.74 in) high, and name it vest_outline. In Advanced Options change the Colour Mode to RGB and click OK. **File > New**

Now place a photograph or scan of half your front and back vest pattern into the document. You can use the images supplied on the website (vest_shape1.jpg and vest_shape2.jpg) or use one of your own.
File > Place

Step 5 (continued)

Select the Pen tool from the Tools panel.

In the Appearance panel click on the right-hand side of the bar next to Fill and click on the down arrow while holding down the Shift key. Select a fill of None.

In the same way, select a stroke of black.

Draw around the outside of one half of the vest pattern.

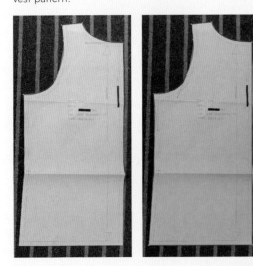

Draw around the second half.

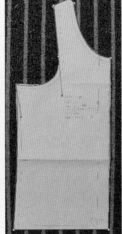

Step 6

To create the full pattern shape for the back and front of your vest at the correct final size, start by turning off Layer 1 in the Layers panel by clicking on the 'eye' icon next to it. Then create a new layer by selecting the icon at the foot of the Layers panel.

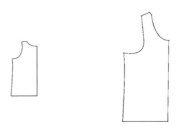

Choose the Selection tool from the Tools panel. Place the back pattern shape in the top left-hand corner of the rectangle.

Holding down the Shift key, drag the bottom left-hand anchor point to the bottom left-hand corner of the rectangle to scale and size the pattern piece proportionally.

Step 6 (continued)

Draw another rectangle and size it with a W value of 254 mm (10 in) and an H value of 573 mm (22.56 in).

Place the front pattern shape in the top right-hand corner and scale in the same way as you did for the back.

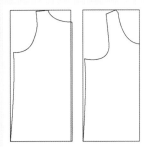

Holding down the Shift key, use the Selection tool to click on the path for the rectangle surrounding the front half of the pattern and the path for the pattern itself, then drag the front of the pattern beneath the back on your artboard.

With the Selection tool, select both sides of the pattern and their rectangular boxes and, holding down the Control key, click the mouse to bring up a menu; select Transform and then Reflect. In the Reflect dialogue box, select Vertical and an angle of 90 degrees. Click Copy.

Step 6 (continued)

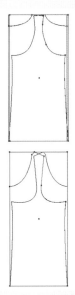

Now, holding down the Shift key and using the Selection tool, select both the right-hand side of the back pattern piece and the rectangle surrounding it. Drag the right-hand piece away from the left and position it so that there is no gap between the actual pattern pieces (you may need to overlap them slightly to ensure that you can join them together successfully later). Repeat for the front pattern piece.

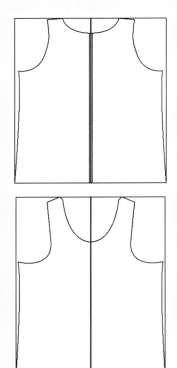

Step 7

To join the two halves of the front and back pattern pieces, start by removing the rectangles surrounding the pieces. Hold down the Shift key and use the Selection tool to select all four rectangles surrounding your pattern pieces. **Edit > Cut**

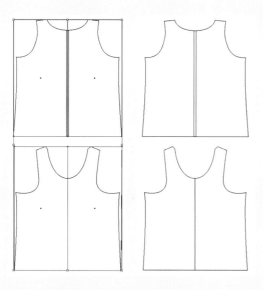

Join the pattern pieces together by choosing **Window > Pathfinder** then **Select > All**

In the Pathfinder panel, select Unite from Shape Modes.

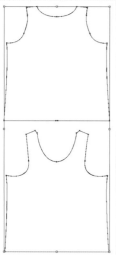

Step 8

Now that you have your complete pattern pieces for the front and back of your vest, you can apply your pebble pattern. In the Swatches panel, click the panel menu icon at the top right. Select **Open Swatch Library > Other Library.**

Browse to find your vest_pattern_swatches.ai file and click Open.

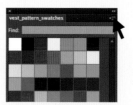

Ensuring you have selected both the back and front pattern pieces with the Selection tool, click on Fill in the Tools panel.

Then choose your new pebble pattern swatch from the Swatches panel. Your pattern pieces will fill with your pebble pattern.

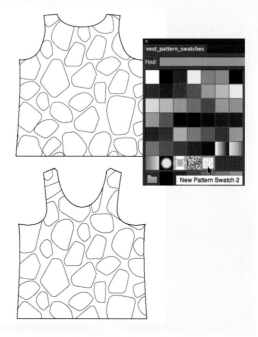

Step 8 (continued)

Finally, change the stroke to 0.05 pt to ensure you have a fine line for the laser-cutting machine. First **Select > All** and then change the width of the stroke in the Control panel.

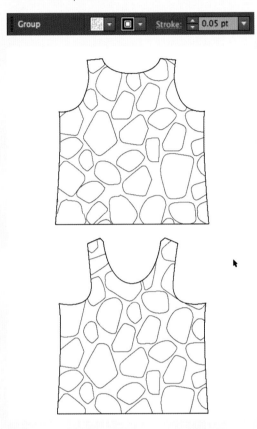

Save as the document as vest_outline.ai.
File > Save As. Alternatively, you can use the file supplied on the website ('vest_outline.ai').

Sewing instructions

Your file is now ready for cutting (see 'Setting up your Illustrator files' on page 12). Here, the pattern motif has been vinyl-cut for heat-transfer application to the final fabric.

Step 1
With right sides facing, sew the front and back pattern pieces together at the shoulders and side seams. Finish the seams if you are using a natural fabric such as cotton or silk. If you are using a polyester or 50 per cent polyester blend, the laser cutter will seal the edges for you, as the polyester will melt and fuse. Finish the armholes and neckline and turn up a double hem. Turn right side out.

Step 2
On your cut vinyl, peel the unwanted background negative away from the pebble shapes that you will be heat-transferring to your vest.

Step 3
Heat-transfer/iron the shapes on to the front of your vest to finish.

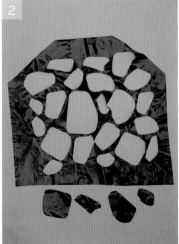

Belt / chevron design

In this tutorial you will learn to:

* create chevron, zigzag and criss-cross
  surface designs;

* make a simple belt pattern;

* laser etch a pattern on to a heavy material such
  as leather, suede or canvas.

The belt shown here was made from ponyskin.
When you are using materials such as ponyskin it is
best to keep your design shapes simple and to work
with contrast instead. Here, dark and light stripes
create a zebra-like chevron pattern.

Step 1

Create a new document with an artboard size of A3 (11.69 x 16.54 in) and name it pattern_template. In Advanced Options change the Colour Mode to RGB and click OK. **File > New**

Use a grid to help you draw and position the lines of the pattern by selecting **View > Show Grid** and then **View > Snap to Grid**.

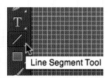

Line Segment Tool

Step 2

To create the first side of the chevron shape, select the Line Segment tool and draw an angled guideline from the top right-hand corner of one square down to the opposite corner at the bottom of the square beneath.

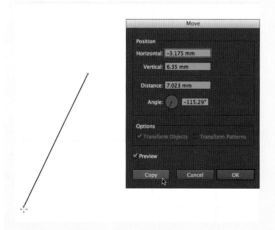

Step 2 (continued)

Draw a vertical line and a horizontal line to create a triangle at the top of your angled guideline.

Join the lines together by first choosing the Selection tool and then, with the Shift key held down, clicking on the vertical and horizontal lines. **Object > Path > Join**

With the lines still selected, press the Control key and click the mouse to bring up a menu; select **Transform > Move**.

In the Move dialogue box, click Preview and then with Horizontal selected, use the arrow keys on the keyboard to move the two sides of the triangle one step to the right. Then select Vertical and use the arrow keys to move the triangle one step down and into position on the diagonal guideline. Click Copy. Press Command+D to duplicate the triangle along the guideline.

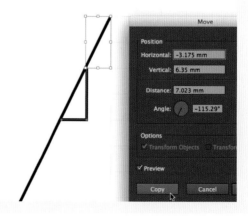

Step 2 (continued)

Remove the angled guideline by first choosing it with the Selection tool then selecting **Edit > Cut.**

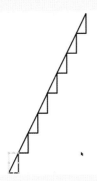

To create the rest of the chevron pattern you need to duplicate this first section then mirror it before creating the second side of the shape. To duplicate and move the line to create the lower half of the chevron, select the new lines that you have made with the Selection tool, hold down the Alt key and drag the lines to the left.

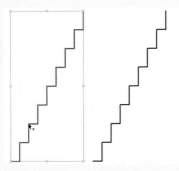

With the duplicated line selected, press the Control key and click the mouse to bring up a menu; select **Transform > Reflect.** In the dialogue box select Horizontal and Preview, then click OK.

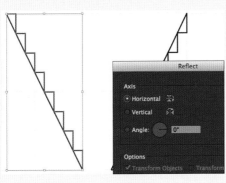

Step 2 (continued)

Now move the lines to create a chevron shape by selecting the lines with the Selection tool and then dragging them so that they sit beneath the first section of the chevron shape.

To create the second side of the shape, select both sets of lines with the Selection tool and drag to the right while holding down the Alt key.

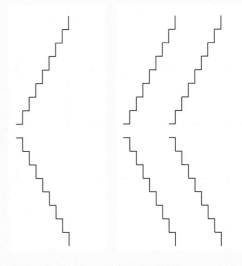

Now join all four sets of lines together to complete the chevron shape. Select the Line Segment tool and draw a line joining the two segments of lines together in the middle. Then draw lines joining the top and bottom of the two shapes together.

Select the whole shape with the Selection tool and then select **Object > Path > Join.** The whole shape is now complete.

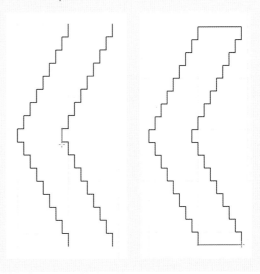

Step 3

Having created the basic chevron shape, you can now use it to create the pattern and then save it in your swatch library. Alternatively, you can use the file supplied on the website ('chevron_template.ai').

Start by clicking Swap Fill and Stroke in the Tools panel so that the fill is black and the stroke is None.

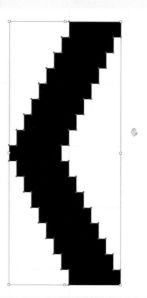

To create the pattern choose **Object > Pattern > Make** and click OK.

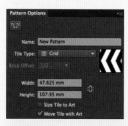

If you then click on the down arrow next to Tile Type in the dialogue box you will see three samples: Grid, Brick by Row and Brick by Column.

Select the pattern you like (here, Grid was selected), then name it New Pattern 2 and click Done in the Control panel. You have created a new pattern in the swatches library.

Click the panel menu icon on the Swatches panel. If you wish to save your template in gradients select Save Swatch Library as AI ... and name it pattern_template_swatches.ai. Or if you wish to save it as a solid colour only, select Save Swatch Library as ASE ... and name it pattern_template.ase. Click Save. You can experiment and make a couple more patterns.

Step 4

Your new patterns in the swatches library can now be used to create the belt. Here, three different belt designs will be decorated with three different laser-cut patterns. You can also add a laser-etch pattern to further enhance the decorative effect. Start by opening the belt_template.ai supplied on the website. **File > Open**

Click the panel menu icon on the Swatches panel. Select Open Swatch Library from the menu and then Other Library ... from the sub-menu.

Open the pattern_template_swatches.ai file to open another swatches library. **File > Open**

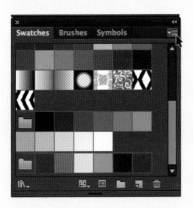

With the Selection tool select the top belt outline.

Select Fill from the Tools panel and then select New Pattern 2 from the second swatches library.

To rescale the pattern within the belt shape press the Control key and click the mouse to bring up a menu. Select **Transform > Scale**. In the dialogue box check Transform Patterns, uncheck Transform Objects and reduce the scale to 50 per cent in Uniform. Click OK.

Press the Control key again and click the mouse to bring up the menu. Select **Transform > Move**. Ensure Transform Patterns is selected and change the values in the dialogue box to align the pattern within the belt template: Horizontal –4 mm (–0.16 in) and Vertical –2 mm (–0.08 in). Click OK.

The pattern should now be the correct size and aligned centrally within the template.

Step 5

You can now use a different pattern on the second belt template. Choose the second belt outline by selecting it with the Selection tool.

Select Fill in the Tools panel and select New Pattern from the second swatches library you opened in Step 4.

Again, you will need to rescale the pattern and align it within your template. Press the Control key and click the mouse to bring up the menu. Select **Transform > Scale**; uncheck Transform Objects, check Transform Patterns and reduce the scale to 25 per cent in Uniform. Click OK.

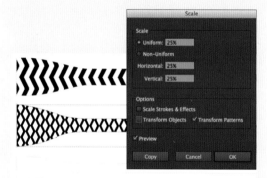

Press the Control key and click the mouse again. Select **Transform > Move** and check that Transform Patterns is selected, then change the values in the dialogue box to Horizontal −3 mm (−0.12 in) and Vertical −41 mm (−1.61 in). Click OK.

Step 6

Repeat the steps above to finish the third belt with another new pattern.

Complete all the patterns on the templates by changing the outline to magenta for an external cut. **Select > All**

Select Stroke in the Tools panel and change the stroke colour to magenta (R:255, G:0 and B:255).

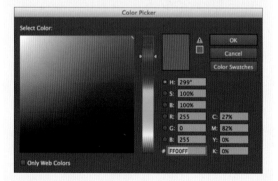

Change the stroke weight to a hairline width of 0.05 pt in the Control panel.

At this stage you can now send the file to the laser-cutting machine. It is set up for the belt shapes to be cut out and for the surface pattern to be applied.

Step 7

You can also add laser-etch embellishments to your patterns before cutting.

Start by selecting **Window > Layers**, then locking the first layer by clicking in the blank box to the right of the 'eye' icon in the Layers panel.

Then create a new layer by clicking the panel menu icon and selecting New Layer. Click OK in the Layer Options menu. Alternatively, you can just select Create New Layer at the foot of the Layers panel. To add further detail to your pattern select the Line Segment tool and select Stroke from the Tools panel. Change the colour of the line to blue in the Colour panel (R:0, G:0 and B:255).

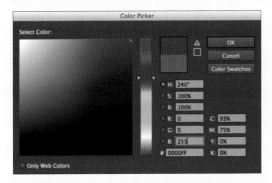

At this stage you might find it easier to zoom in on your pattern using the Zoom tool in the Tools panel. Draw a line on your pattern using the Line Segment tool and then choose the Selection tool. Duplicate the line by first selecting it and then pressing the Alt key while dragging the line. Continue to duplicate the line down the chevron shape.

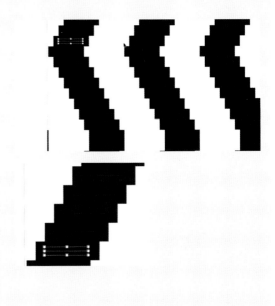

Once you have finished, you can then duplicate the lines across the rest of your chevron pattern. With the Selection tool, select all the lines.

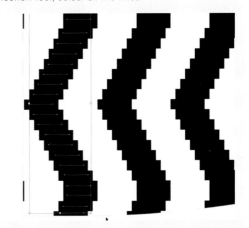

Select **Object > Group** then press the Control key and click the mouse to bring up the menu. Select **Transform > Move** and change the distance to 23.8 mm (0.94 in) in the dialogue box. This time check Transform Objects and uncheck Transform Patterns. Click OK.

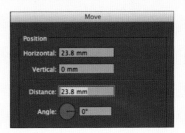

Step 7 (continued)

Select the lines with the Selection tool and either hold down the Alt key while dragging the selection to the next chevron shape, or press Command+D to repeat across the whole of the belt shape.

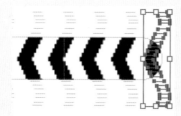

Since you have repeated the whole selection across the belt, there will now be some lines outside the outline of your template. To remove them, select the Eraser tool from the Tools panel and use it to clean up the lines that are not needed.

Step 7 (continued)

When you have erased the lines outside the template, you have finished. The new lines will create an etched effect within the design.

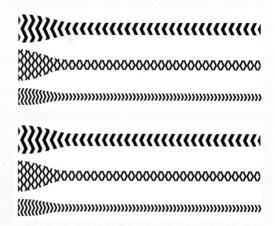

Save the file as belts.ai. **File > Save As**
Alternatively, you can use the file supplied on the website ('belts_template.ai').

Assembly instructions

Laser cut two of each belt pattern so that you can join them together at the centre front to create the final belt. You will also need to cut a plain belt template shape to line the back of the belt. You can use ponyskin for this project (A), and a plain leather or suede for the back lining of the belt (B). Alternatively, you could cut the belt-backing shape from a heavy material such as canvas. We have used a leather backing and stitched around the belt shape with an industrial sewing machine, but you can also attach the plain backing with leather glue.

Step 1

To mark out where you will attach the snap fasteners, or Sam Brownes (peg-shaped fasteners), that will join the belt together, put the belt around your waist and bring the ends of it back towards the front – they should cross over at the centre back and reach around to your sides. Make a mark where you want to attach the fastener at each side. You will need to use a leather hole-puncher to create two holes on each side of the belt – one at the end of the belt and one at the point at which it reaches the side.

Step 2

Insert the side of the fastener with the flat plate through from the under side to the upper side of the belt at the sides.

Screw the other side of the fastener in place. You can now wear the belt, slotting the rounded end of the stud through the hole at the end of the belt on each side.

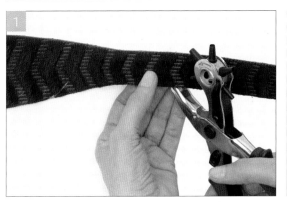

iPad case / net design

This tutorial demonstrates how to:

* create a two-tone effect using a double
  layer of different-coloured substrates;

* make a pattern for an iPad case.

You can use a variety of materials for this project,
including neoprene or faux suede. The case shown in
the main picture uses leather and suede in two colours,
layered together to create a contrast between the laser
cut and the lining. The variation shown below right uses
a different surface design, laser etched (rather than cut)
on to a thicker leather.

Step 1

First draw one half of your design on graph paper at full size (1:1 scale). You can also use the outline provided on the website (iPad-drawing.jpg). Scan your drawing in at a resolution of 300dpi.

Step 2

Create a new document with an artboard size of 1000 mm (39.37 in) wide and 420 mm (16.54 in) high and name it iPad_outline. In Advanced Options change the Colour Mode to RGB and click OK. **File > New.**

Select **File > Place** to import your file.

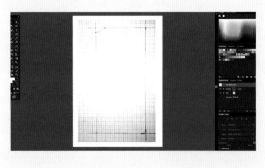

Lock the layer by opening up the Layers panel and clicking the blank box next to the 'eye' icon. **Window > Layers**

To make a new layer to draw over the template drawing, click the panel menu icon in the upper-right corner of the Layers panel menu and select New Layer. In the Layer Options dialogue box name it Layer 2 and click OK. **Layers > New Layer > OK**

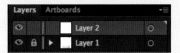

Step 3

Next, position a guide to help you create the ellipse shape at the top of the case. First select Layer 2 in the Layers panel. Then use the rulers to help position the guide. **View > Rulers > Show Rulers**

Click on the ruler at the left-hand side of the screen and drag the guide to left-hand line of your drawing. **View > Snap to Point**

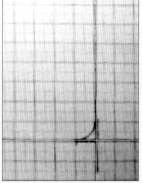

Step 4

Now draw around the outline of your iPad case design by selecting the Rectangle tool and then clicking and dragging over the rectangular shape of your drawing.

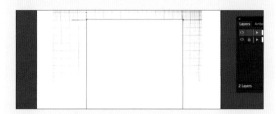

To remove the fill from inside the rectangle, open the Colour panel by selecting **Window > Colour**, then click on the icon at the top left to change the fill to None.

Step 5

Next, create a rounded corner at the bottom of the
case. Select the Ellipse tool, hold down the Shift
key and draw a circle. Using the Selection tool, click
on the edge of the circle and move and snap it
to the bottom right-hand corner of your rectangle.

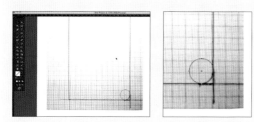

Step 6

Now create a similar shape at the opening of the case.
Select the Ellipse tool again, but this time without
the Shift key, and draw an ellipse shape. Using the
Selection tool, move and snap its centre point to the
top left-hand corner of your rectangle.

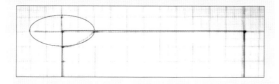

Then hide the background layer so that just your
outline is visible, making it easier to see, by clicking
the eye icon to the left of Layer 1 in the Layers panel.

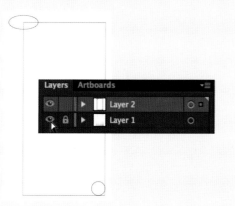

Step 7

Now isolate the outline of the iPad case so that all the
extraneous lines can be deleted. **Window >
Pathfinder**

Select all the objects by choosing the Selection tool
and clicking and dragging around all of them.

In the Pathfinder panel select Pathfinders,
then Divide.

Click outside the objects with the Selection tool so
that they are deselected.

Zoom in with the Magnify tool, then choose the Direct
Selection tool. Click on the pathways of the shapes/
strokes you do not want and press the Backspace key
after each selection until they are all removed. (You
can also use **Edit > Cut** or Command+X to delete.)
Click outside the shapes between each selection
to deselect.

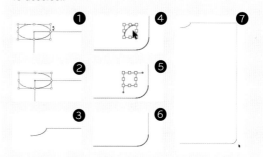

Step 8

To make the stitch holes, you will need some guides to work to. **View > Show Grid**

Choose the Ellipse tool and, holding down the Shift key, make a circle of approximately 1 mm (0.04 in) in diameter. You can size the circle in the Control panel at the top of your screen.

Select the circle using the Selection tool and move it to the top left of your iPad case.

Hold down the Control key and click the mouse in the circle to bring up a menu. Select **Transform > Move**, then in the Move dialogue box enter a horizontal value of 0 mm (0 in) and a vertical value of 5 mm (0.20 in). Choose a distance of 5 mm (0.20 in) and an angle of -90 degrees, then click Copy.

Press Command+D repeatedly to build up a vertical line of circles until you reach the bottom of the iPad case.

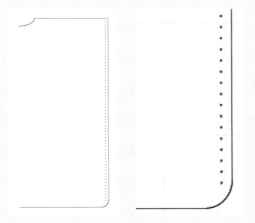

Step 9

To turn the corner, select the last circle using the Selection tool, then select the Alt key to make a new circle. Drag this new circle and position it to follow the curve at the bottom corner of the case.

Continue making new circles until you reach the horizontal line at the bottom of the case.

Hold down the Control key and click the mouse in the first circle at the bottom, then select **Transform > Move**. In the Move dialogue box enter a horizontal value of -5 mm (-0.20 in) and a vertical value of 0 mm (0 in). Choose a distance of 5 mm (0.20 in) and an angle of 180 degrees. Click Copy.

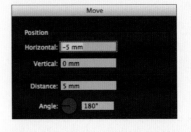

Press Command+D repeatedly to build up a horizontal line of circles.

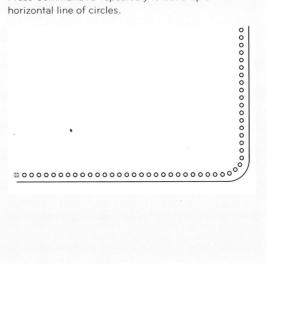

Step 10

To start creating the full shape of the iPad case, first duplicate the shape.

Select > All

Object > Group

Click on the outline of the shape and hold down the Alt key while dragging the shape to duplicate the complete outline and create two sides of the iPad case.

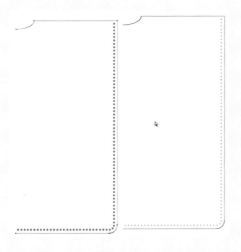

Now hold down the Control key, click in the selection and choose **Transform > Reflect** from the menu. In the Reflect dialogue box select Vertical and an angle of 90 degrees. Click OK.

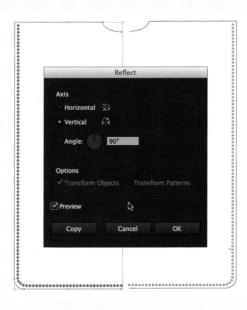

Step 11

To complete the shape of the iPad case, drag and join the two sides together to make the complete outline.

Save the iPad_outline file as an .ai Illustrator file. **File > Save As**. Alternatively, you can use the file supplied on the website ('iPad_outline.ai').

Step 12

Having created your outline, you can now add the design for the laser cut or etch to the template. You can either use one of the templates from the website or create your own (see steps 1–4 of the Vest project, pages 16–19, for the method). Here, we will use the net design from the website.

Open up a new document with an artboard size of 1000 mm (39.37 in) wide and 420 mm (16.54 in) high, and name it iPad_case. In Advanced Options change the Colour Mode to RGB and click OK. **File > New**

Open the net_pattern.ai file from the website. **File > Open**

Open the iPad_outline.ai file. **File > Open**

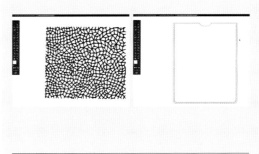

You will now have three documents open.

Step 13

Select the New Project file, then copy the outline of the iPad case and copy it into 'iPad_case'.
Select > All, Edit > Copy, Edit > Paste

Step 14 (continued)

Paste the outline shape of the right-hand side of the iPad case back into the document and, using the Selection tool, move it close to the stitch holes on the right-hand side of the case. **Edit > Paste**

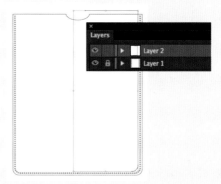

Step 14

Next, set up a placeholder for the net design on top of the outline.

With the Selection tool, double-click the outline shape of the iPad case on the right-hand side, but do not select the stitch holes; Layer 1 <Group> will appear at the top left of the screen. Click the outline shape once again to select it, and copy. **Edit > Copy**

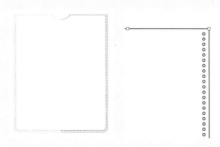

Go back two levels by clicking on the arrow at the top left of the document twice until all the layers disappear.

Open up a new layer. **Window > Layers**

Click the panel menu icon in the upper-right corner of the Layers panel menu and select New Layer. In the Layer Options panel, name it Layer 2 and click OK.

Lock Layer 1 by selecting it in the Layers panel and clicking the blank box next to the eye icon.

Duplicate one more outline shape by clicking on the outline shape and holding down the Alt key while dragging to the left.

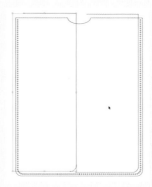

Hold down the Control key, click in this second outline shape and choose **Transform > Reflect** from the menu. In the Reflect dialogue box select Vertical, and enter an angle of 90 degrees.

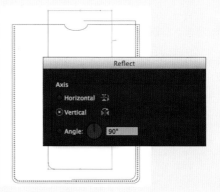

Step 14 (continued)

With the Selection tool, move the second outline shape to the left-hand side of the case, close to the stitch holes.

To recreate the thumb notch at the top of the case, select the Ellipse tool. Draw an ellipse and place it in the centre of the opening between the two sides of the placeholder shape that you have created.

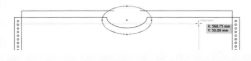

Select the Line Segment tool and draw a line from the top left of the placeholder shape, just below the top stitch hole, to the top right.

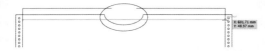

Step 15

Having created the placeholder shape you can now paste the net design on to your iPad case. First create a new layer by clicking the panel menu icon in the upper-right corner of the Layers panel menu and selecting New Layer. In the Layer Options panel, name it Layer 3 and click OK. Select Layer 3 by clicking on its name in the Layers panel.

Go to the 'net_pattern.ai' document and copy and paste the design into Layer 3 of 'iPad_case.ai'.

Select > All, Edit > Copy, Edit > Paste

Increase the size of the net design so that it covers the outline of your iPad case. With the Selection tool, click on the bottom right-hand corner of the net design and, while holding down the Shift key, drag the corner of the bounding box to transform the scale and increase the size of the design.

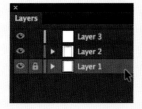
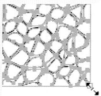

Step 15 (continued)

Then, with the Selection tool, move the design until it fits over the outline. Click outside the net design to deselect.

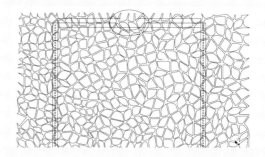

Now tidy up the design so that the net pattern fits just within the placeholder. You can do this by dividing the net design and removing the extraneous lines around the edge of the placeholder shape. **Select > All** (which will just select Layers 2 and 3 because Layer 1 is still locked).

Select **Window > Pathfinder**. In the Pathfinder panel select Divide from Pathfinders.

View > Outline
With the Direct Selection tool hold down the Shift key and click and drag around each side of the outline of the placeholder in turn. After each selection, cut away the outside of the design. Click outside the iPad case shape between each selection to deselect. **Edit > Cut**

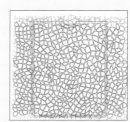
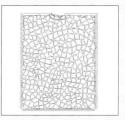

Step 15 (continued)

Now zoom in with the Zoom tool. Use the Direct Selection tool to tidy up the outside of the placeholder shape by clicking on the areas you do not want and using **Edit > Cut** to delete them. (You can also use the Backspace key or Command+X to delete.) Again, click outside the shapes between each selection to deselect. You also need to delete the edges of the placeholder shape where they cut across the pattern. Make sure you also delete all the anchor points, too

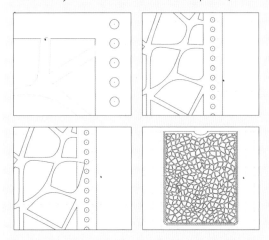

Click outside the outline of the case with the Selection tool to deselect. Select Layer 3 and expand the layer by clicking on the arrow buttons to reveal the paths within the layer. Select the path named Compound Path and delete it by dragging it into the Trash Can. This will get rid of any double lines previously created automatically by the Image Trace used when the net_pattern.ai file was originally made.

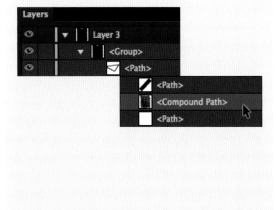

Unlock Layer 1 by clicking the padlock icon next to the eye icon in the Layers panel.

Step 16

Now change the colour of the net pattern in Layer 3 to differentiate this as an internal cut for the laser-cutting machine.

Select the net pattern with the Selection tool.

Select **Window > Colour** and select Stroke. In the Colour panel select green from the rainbow bar and then change the sliders to R:0, G:255 and B:0.

View > Preview
Now change the colour of the stitch holes, starting with the left-hand side of the case. Select Layer 1 in the Layers panel and expand the layer by clicking on the arrow button. Select the <Group> with the stitch holes on the left-hand side.

Using the Selection tool double-click on the left-hand side of the iPad case; Layer 1 <Group> will appear in the top left of the screen. Then select the left-hand side of the case with the Selection tool; the outline and the stitch holes will be selected. Finally, click on the outline of the iPad case to deselect it, leaving only the stitch holes selected.

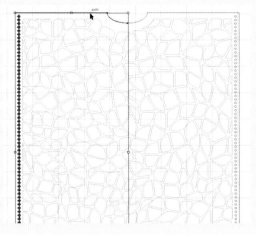

Step 16 (continued)

Window > Colour

Repeat the previous steps to colour the stitch holes green (R:0, G:255 and B:0) for an internal cut.

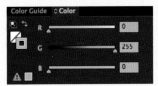

Remaining in Layer 1, select the <Group> in the Layers panel for the outline of the ipad and change the colour to magenta for an external cut:
R: 255 G:0 B: 255

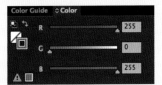

Now click the arrow at the top left of the Control panel (Back one level) and leave the Group.

Click the arrow again to Exit Isolation Mode.

 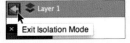

Select the right side of the iPad case and repeat the whole process for colouring the stitch holes and outline. To finish **Select > All then Object > Group**.

Step 16 (continued)

Duplicate one more side of the iPad case by holding down the Alt key and clicking and dragging the outside edge so that you have a Front and a Back. Finally, save the iPad_case file. **File > Save As** Alternatively, you can use the file supplied on the website ('iPad_case.ai').

Back side   Front side

Sewing instructions

Stitch the iPad pieces together with approximately 2m (6½ ft) of lanyard or leather. You could also use plastic lacing. The technician will probably apply a protective backing to the leather for cutting. Peel this backing off the laser-cut leather before you begin.

Step 1
Tie a knot at one end of your lanyard and thread it through the first hole at the top of the iPad case, passing from the wrong side to the right side.

Step 2
Using a running stitch, sew the two pieces of leather together through the laser-cut holes.

Step 3
Sandwich the ends of the lanyard between the two sides of the iPad case, then secure them with glue.

To create a two-tone contrasting case, use the iPad template to make two more sides, but this time cutting only the stitch holes. Use a finer, contrasting fabric, such as suede. Sandwich these pieces inside the two laser-cut sides before stitching together.

Skirt / lace pattern

This tutorial demonstrates:

* how to apply your own hand-drawn design to your
  substrate by means of laser-cut or as a laser-etch;

* how to create a broderie anglaise lace pattern;

* the process of creating a skirt with almost
  no sewing (with the exception of one button).

You could use a variety of fabrics for this project
depending on your budget. A light, soft leather or suede
is a good substrate for a laser-etch (used for the black
skirt shown below right), and a heavy habotai silk lends
itself well to a laser-cut (below left and main picture).
For this garment, choose a material that drapes nicely.

Step 1

Draw the outline of one side of your skirt at any size. The drawing here was made on pattern paper. (This is also provided as a jpeg on the website: 'skirt_outline.jpg')

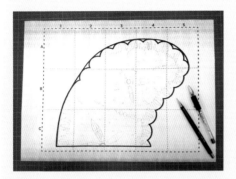

Step 2

Next, add the lace pattern. Scan your drawing with the lace pattern and open it in Photoshop.

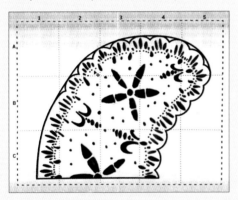

To tidy up the drawing, first enhance the contrast of your image. **Image > Adjustments > Levels**

Drag the left-hand and the right-hand slider into the centre of the Levels dialogue box, then click OK.

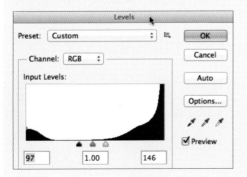

Step 3

Use the Eraser tool to clean up the image. You can adjust the eraser by opening the Brush preset picker in the Control panel and selecting the size and hardness.

Click and drag the eraser to clean up the image.

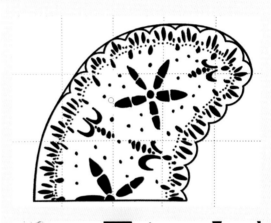

Step 4

Next, isolate the shape of your skirt by removing the area outside the outline, in this case the grid. Use the Quick Selection tool and the Tool preset picker in the Control panel to choose Add to Selection.

Click and drag the Quick Selection tool around the outside of your drawing. **Edit > Cut** to remove the selected areas.

Step 5

To ensure that you do not have a double line around your laser-cut drawing, erase the outside edge of your drawing using the Eraser tool. Again, you can adjust the eraser by opening the Brush preset picker in the Control panel and selecting the size and hardness. **File > Save As** and name it lace_pattern.jpg. Alternatively, use the lace_pattern.jpg provided on the website.

Select JPEG from the drop-down menu and in the dialogue box select Maximum Quality and Baseline ('Standard').

Step 6

To import the lace_pattern.jpg into Illustrator, first open up a new document, with an artboard size of A3 (11.69 x 16.54 in), and name it lace_etch/cut.ai. In Advanced Options change the Colour Mode to RGB and click OK. **File > New**

Place the lace_pattern.jpg file in this document. **File > Place**

To trace your drawing, first select the image with the Direct Selection tool.

To transform the file into a vector file suitable for laser cutting use the Image Trace feature. **Object > Image Trace > Make and Expand**

Using the Selection Tool, select the object and double-click. This will remove the negative line created in the Image Trace feature.

Check that at the top left of your document you can see Layer 1 <Group>.

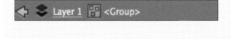

Using the Selection tool, select the path on the top edge of the frame and drag it to the right.

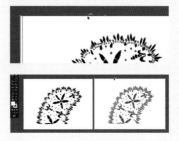

Step 7

Now create a file for laser etching (using the left-hand copy of the lace pattern) and a file for laser cutting (using the right-hand copy), starting with the laser-cut file. To delete any double lines that automatically occur during the Image Trace function, you will need to ensure you are working in the right layer at any one time.

Double-click the object on the right-hand side; check that at the top left of your document you can see Layer 1 <Group> <Compound Path>.

Using the Selection Tool, select the outline path of the object on the right side.

Edit > Cut

Step 7 (continued)

Click the arrow (Back one level) in the Control panel at the top of the document once; you should now see Layer 1 <Group>. Select the object on the right-hand side again.

Edit > Cut

Now step back to the base layer by clicking the arrow at the top left of the Control panel until the bar has disappeared.

 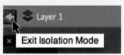

Paste the object back on the right-hand side. You can press the Command key and drag the object to the right using the Selection tool if necessary.
Edit > Paste

Step 7 (continued)

Now change the stroke in preparation for the laser cut. Select **Window > Appearance** to open the Appearance panel.

Select Fill by clicking on the right-hand side of the bar. Click on the down arrow while holding down the Shift key. Select a fill of None.

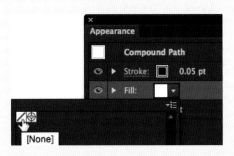

Select Stroke by clicking on the right-hand side of the bar. Click the down arrow (but this time do not hold down the Shift key). Select black.

Input the hairline stroke weight of 0.05 pt.

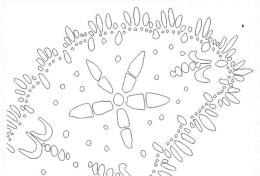

Step 8

Now create the laser etch using the object on the left. Select it using the Selection tool and open the Appearance panel. **Window > Appearance**

Click the panel menu icon in the upper right-hand corner and select Add New Fill. Click the down arrow while holding down the Shift key. Select black.

You now have a pattern for laser cutting on the left and for laser etching (engraving) on the right.

Save the lace_etch/cut file as an Illustrator file.
File > Save As
Alternatively, use the 'lace_etch/cut.ai' file provided on the website.

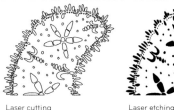

Laser cutting   Laser etching (engraving)

Step 9

Now we are going to create a new pattern template for the skirt on which to position the laser etch or cut that we have just created.

Create a new document with an artboard size of 500 mm (19.69 in) wide and 500 mm (19.69 in) high, and name it lace_outline. In Advanced Options change the Colour Mode to RGB and click OK. **File > New**

Place your original hand-drawing template from Step 1 (skirt_outline) into the document in order to trace over it. **File > Place**

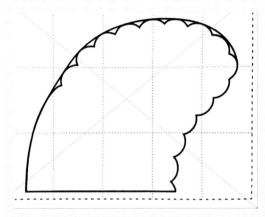

Lock this first layer by clicking the blank box next to the 'eye' icon in the Layers panel. **Window > Layers**

Create a new layer by clicking on the panel menu icon in the upper right-hand corner of the Layers panel. Select **Layers > New Layer** and click OK.

In the Layer Options dialogue box name it Layer 2 and click OK.

Step 10

Now trace around the outline of the skirt manually.

Select the Pen tool. Choose a fill of None and a stroke of black in the Appearance panel, and draw around the outline of the skirt with the Pen tool.

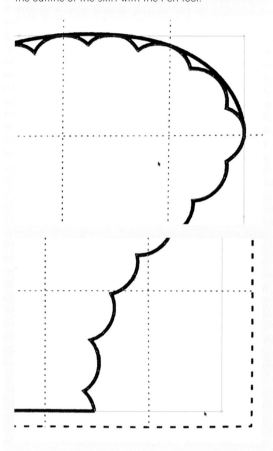

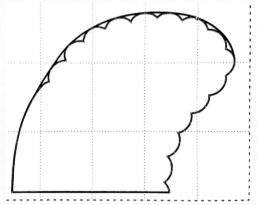

Step 11

Create a new document in the correct scale to make a one-size skirt with movable buttonhole – 114 cm (44.88 in) wide and 76 cm (29.92 in) high – and name it skirt_template. In Advanced Options change the Colour Mode to RGB and click OK. **File > New**. This is also provided on the website: skirt_template.ai

Return to your lace_outline document to copy the outline. Select the drawing with the Selection tool then **Edit > Copy**.

Now return to your new skirt_template document and paste in the outline by selecting **Edit > Paste**.

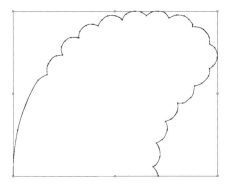

Step 12

To create and position the pattern of the whole skirt on the screen we first need to rotate the outline of half of the skirt and then copy and mirror it, before joining the two sides together to create the complete shape.

Select the outline in your new file. **Select > All** Press the Control key and click the mouse to bring up a menu; select **Transform > Rotate**. In the dialogue box change the angle to 90 degrees and click OK.

To copy one side of the skirt, select the outline path with the Selection tool, hold down the Alt key and drag to create a copy.

Step 12 (continued)

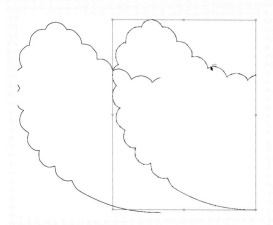

Keeping this second half of the outline selected, press the Control key, click the mouse again and this time select **Transform > Reflect**. In the dialogue box change the angle to 90 degrees, select Vertical and click OK.

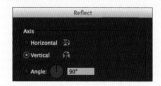

Join the two sides together by dragging with the Selection tool.

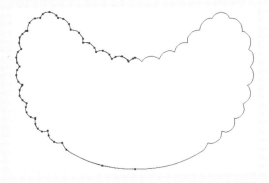

Select > All

Object > Group

Finally, keeping the outline selected, change the stroke to 0.05 pt in the Control panel.

Step 13

Now add your pattern to the skirt outline as a separate layer.

First lock this outline layer by clicking the blank box next to the eye icon in the Layers menu.

Make a new layer by clicking the panel menu icon in the upper right-hand corner of the Layers panel. Select New Layer from the menu, name it Layer 2 and click OK.

Return to your original document, lace_etch/cut.ai, and copy the laser cut or etch by selecting it with the Selection tool.

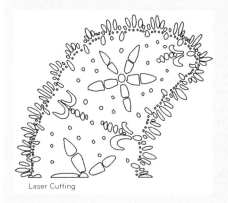

Laser Cutting

Edit > Copy
Return to your skirt_template document and paste in the laser or etch pattern. **Edit > Paste**

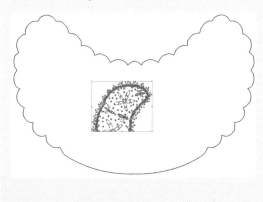

Step 13 (continued)

Now repeat the sequence given in Step 12 to rotate and reflect the pattern.

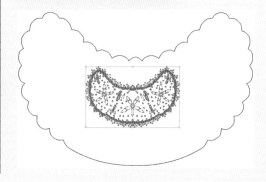

Step 14

Resize the lace pattern within the template. Select **View > Rulers > Show Rulers** to see the size of your object in the document window.

To resize, select a corner of the frame of the object; using Command and Shift, rescale it by eye. You can also measure the width of the lace outline using the Measure tool, which you can find by expanding the Eyedropper tool. With the Measure tool selected, position the cursor on one edge of the image and drag to the other side of it. The Information menu will appear and this will show you the width and height of the area that you have measured.

Once you have measured the outline, using the Command and Shift keys, drag a corner of the laser/etch until the width measurement in the Information menu will fit within the outline.

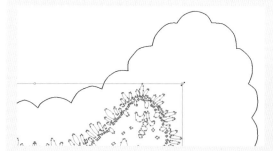

Step 14 (continued)

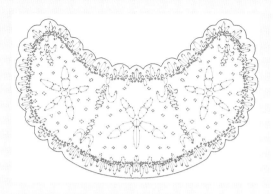

In the Appearance panel, colour the stroke of the lace pattern a different colour to the outline shape in order to signify an internal cut for the laser machine.

Save the file as skirt_template, as an Illustrator eps or ai file. **File > Save As**

Sewing instructions

Step 1
To finish your skirt, wrap around your waist to overlap and let the scalloped edge drape.

Step 2
Mark a closure spot on the fabric where the two edges meet with a pin. Sew a button on the marked spot. Cut a small slit in your fabric for the buttonhole. You now have a finished skirt.

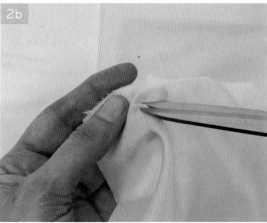

Necklaces / cutting and etching

This tutorial will teach you how to:

* work with a solid substrate to create wearable accessories;

* design, cut and join solid shapes;

* apply your chosen laser-etch design to a solid substrate.

In this tutorial you will create three different necklaces with pendants. You can reuse the geometric design you will create for the Bangle (see pages 94–105) for parts of this tutorial, if you wish. The materials used here are acrylic, wood and ChromaLuxe®, a coated material designed for heat-transfer printing.

Interconnecting laser-cut circle necklace

For this project you can use the file provided on the website, circle_necklace.ai, and move straight to the making instructions on page 61.

Step 1

Create a new document with an artboard size of 2000 mm (78.74 in) wide and 2000 mm (78.74 in) high, and name it circle_necklace.ai. In Advanced Options change the Colour Mode to RGB and click OK. **File > New**
Start by creating one side of your seven-circle pendant. When it is complete, you can mirror it to create the other side.
Select the Ellipse tool from the Tools panel. Also in the Tools panel, select Stroke and change the sliders in the Colour panel to magenta for an external cut on the laser-cutting machine (R:255, G:0 and B:255).

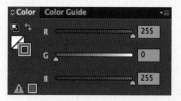

In the Appearance panel change the stroke weight to 1 pt by clicking in the space to the right of the Stroke icon. Enter the new stroke value. Then click in the space next to the Fill icon before holding down the Shift key and clicking the arrow to select a fill of None.

Draw an ellipse and change both the W value and the H value in the Control panel to 65 mm (2.56 in) each to form a circle.

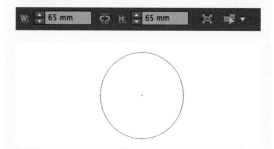

Step 1 (continued)

Select the Selection tool from the Tools panel and, holding down the Alt key, select and drag the circle to duplicate it, positioning the second circle so that it interconnects with the first one. Repeat to create a third circle.

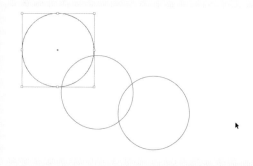

Then repeat to create a fourth circle.

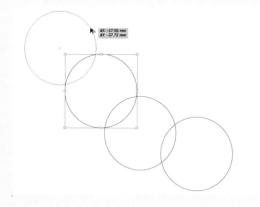

Step 2

Next, you will need to create the holes through which you will link the circles together.
Click outside the circles to deselect them. Select the Ellipse tool again. Choose Stroke from the Tools panel and change the sliders in the Colour panel to green for an internal cut on the laser-cutting machine (R:0, G:255 and B:0).

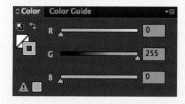

Step 2 (continued)

In the Appearance panel choose a stroke weight of 1 pt and a fill of None (see Step 1).

Draw an ellipse and change both the W value and the H value in the Control panel to 2 mm (0.08 in) each to form a circle.

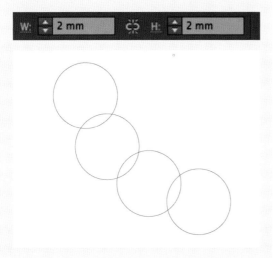

Step 3

Now move the small green circles so that they can be used to join the magenta circles together.
Select the green circle with the Selection tool from the Tools panel and move it to the intersection between the top two circles. Then, holding down the Alt key, select this first circle and drag to duplicate it, positioning in the next intersection. Repeat to add a green circle to the third intersection.

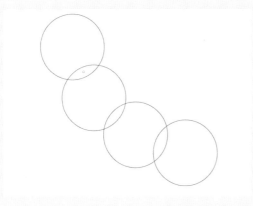

Step 3 (continued)

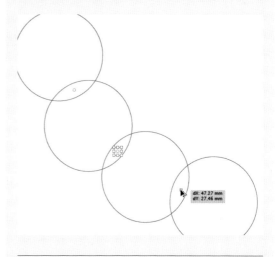

Duplicate a fourth circle and add it to the top of the first circle.

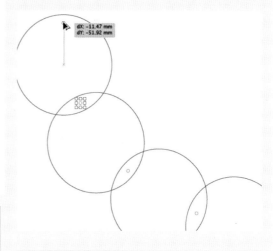

Next, duplicate three circles and move them so that they sit on the other side of the intersections.

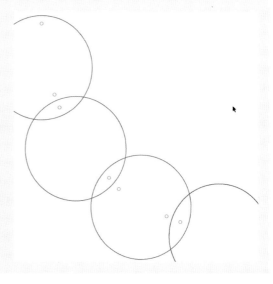

Step 4

Now duplicate and mirror all the green and magenta circles to create the second side of your pendant. **Select > All**

Hold down the Control key, click the mouse to bring up a menu and select Transform > Reflect. In the Reflect dialogue box, select Vertical and an angle of 90 degrees. Tick Preview and then click Copy.

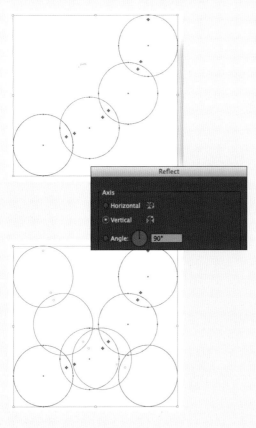

Using the Selection tool, drag the second set of circles to the right, positioning the centre circles on top of each other to create a semicircular shape.

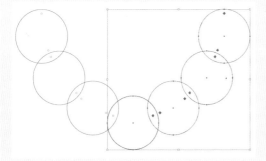

Step 4 (continued)

Select the centre circle and **Edit > Cut** to remove the extra intersecting circle.

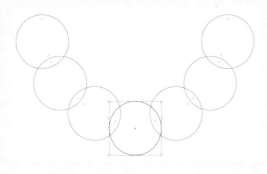

Next create a second semicircle. **Select > All** and then, holding down the Alt key, select the group of circles with the Selection tool and drag the new set beneath the first. Click outside the circles.

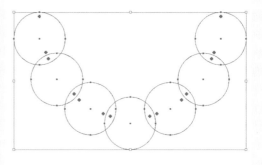

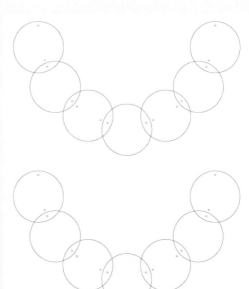

Step 5

Now you need to remove the intersecting points to create a set of shapes that will fit next to each other rather than overlapping.
Select the top left-hand magenta circle from the first semicircular shape and then, holding down the Shift key, select the other magenta circles, avoiding the green circles.

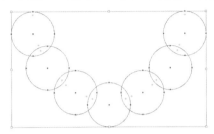

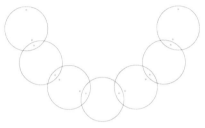

To remove the intersecting areas, choose **Window > Pathfinder** and then click Divide from Pathfinders in the Pathfinder panel.

Double-click on path around the top left-hand circle. Layer 1 <Group> will appear at the top left of the screen.

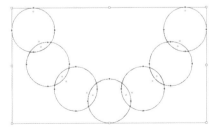

Step 5 (continued)

Select the centre circle and **Edit > Cut** to remove the extra intersecting circle.

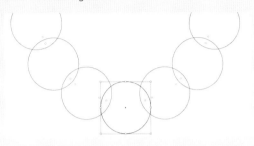

Select circles 2, 4 and 6 (every other circle) with the Selection tool.

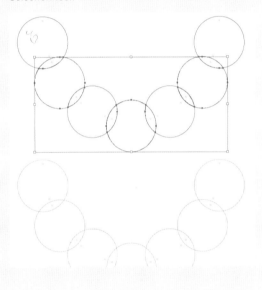

Holding down the Shift key, click on the path of each shape that you want to remove. Then select **Edit > Cut** to remove these three circles and the intersections with the other four circles.

Step 5 (continued)

Finally, click once on the arrow (Back one level) on the top left of the screen, and then click again to Exit Isolation Mode.

Now hold down the Shift key and select circles 1, 3, 5 and 7 from the second semicircular shape.

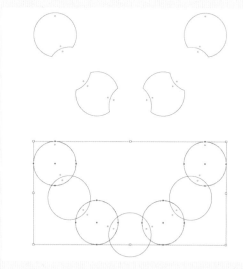

Select **Edit > Cut** to delete, leaving three circles that will fit in the spaces left in the first semicircular shape.

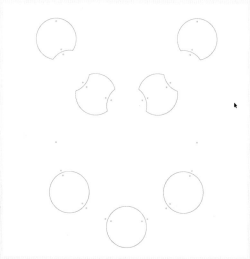

Step 5 (continued)

Once again, hold down the Shift key and select all the green circles outside the magenta circles.

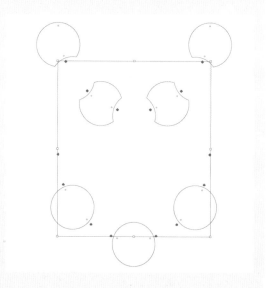

Select **Edit > Cut** to delete them, leaving just the green circles inside the magenta circles through which you can thread jewellery chain links to join the remaining shapes together. (Links can be bought from a specialist supplier or craft shop.)

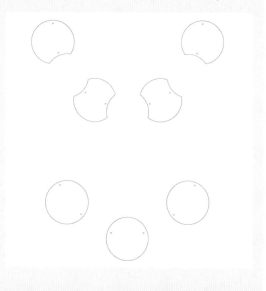

Finally, **Select > All** and change the stroke weight of the circles to 0.05 pt in the Control panel to create a finer cutting line for the laser-cutting machine. Save the file as circle_necklace.ai. **File > Save As**

Making instructions

Step 1
Laser cut your pieces from acrylic and join them together with your chosen metal links.

Step 2
Remove the backing from the acrylic pieces.

Step 3
Insert the final link into the last acrylic circle and attach the chain to finish your pendant necklace.

Note
Experiment to identify the correct length of chain to achieve the best fall of the necklace. You can use an adjustable chain with a small button or ring near the clasp that allows you to make it longer or shorter. The positioning of the links must be accurate in order for the pieces to hang in a smooth curve.

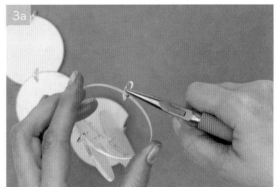

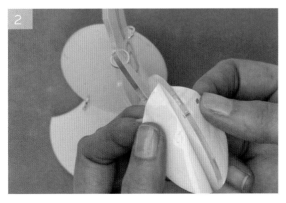

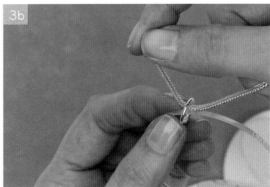

Transfer-print and laser-cut pendant with gem motif

In this tutorial you will create a gem-motif pendant with a trompe-l'oeil print of a vintage pendant.

Step 1

Create a new document with an artboard size of 2000 mm wide (78.74 in) and 2000 mm (78.74 in) high, and name it transfer_pendant.ai. In Advanced Options change the Colour Mode to RGB and click OK.

File > New

Next place the piece of jewellery whose shape you wish to draw around into the document. You can use the photo of the jewel pendant provided on the website (jewels.psd), or create your own. **File > Place**

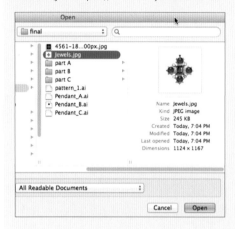

Select **Window > Layers** to open the Layers panel, and lock Layer 1 by clicking the blank box next to the 'eye' icon.

Click the icon at the bottom of the Layers panel to create Layer 2.

Step 2

To begin to draw around the shape of the pendant jewel, first drag a guideline to the centre of the jewel. This will enable you to mirror the shape later. Select **View > Rulers > Show Rulers** and drag a guideline across.

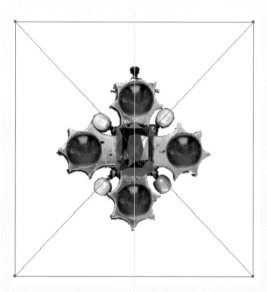

Select the Pen tool from the Tools panel. In the Tools panel select Stroke and change the sliders to magenta in the Colour panel (R:255, G:0 and B:255).

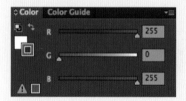

In the Appearance panel change the stroke weight to 1 pt by clicking in the space to the right of the Stroke icon. Enter the new stroke value. Then click in the space next to the Fill icon before holding down the Shift key and clicking the arrow next to it and selecting a fill of None.

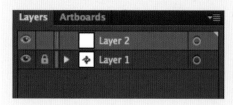

Step 2 (continued)

Now draw around the edge of pendant shape with the Pen tool, starting from the centre guideline at the bottom and working up around the left-hand side until you get to the centre at the top.

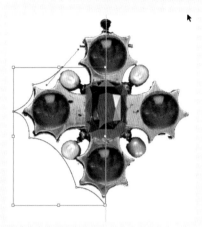

To save drawing around the second side, and to ensure your drawing is symmetrical, choose the Selection tool from the Tools panel and then select your drawing.

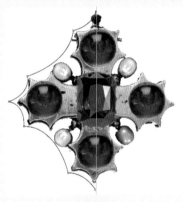

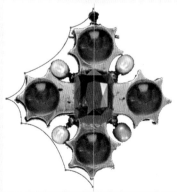

Step 2 (continued)

Hold down the Control key and click the mouse to bring up a menu; select **Transform > Reflect**. In the Reflect dialogue box, select Vertical and an angle of 90 degrees. Tick Preview and click Copy. This will create a duplicate but mirrored copy of the left-hand side.

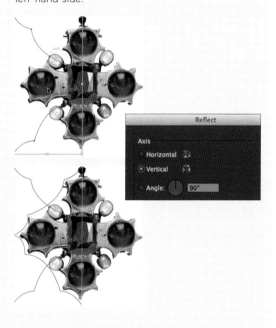

Click on the duplicated side of your drawing with the Selection tool and drag it to the other side of the guideline, lining it up with the left-hand side.

You now need to join the two sides together. Click outside your drawing and then **Select > All**. Choose **Window > Pathfinder** and select Unite from Shape Modes in the Pathfinder panel.

Step 3

Now create a hole at the top of your pendant through which to thread a chain, ribbon or leather cord. Select the Ellipse tool from the Tools panel and then select Stroke. In the Colour panel, change the sliders to green (R:0, G:255 and B:0).

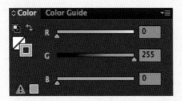

In the Appearance panel, change the stroke weight to 1 pt and select a fill of None (see Step 2).

Draw a circle at the top of pendant placed centrally over the guideline.

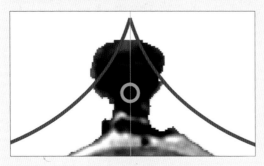

In the Control panel change both the W value and the H value to 3 mm (0.12in).

Step 4

Now hide the background layer so that just your outline is visible, making it easier to see, by clicking the eye icon to the left of Layer 1 in the Layers panel.

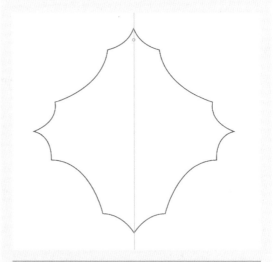

Finally, save your file as transfer-pendant.ai
File > Save As.
Alternatively, you can use the file provided on the website, transfer-pendant.ai

Making instructions

You can now laser cut your pendant and then print the motif design ready for heat-transferring on to your substrate. You can then use a link and chain or leather yarn, even ribbon, to thread through the pendant in order to finish your necklace.

Step 1
Print your motif design on to adhesive heat-transfer paper. Cut your pendant shape and then heat-transfer the design on to the acrylic.

Step 2
Insert a ring through the hole at the top of the pendant.

Step 3
Thread a chain through the ring to complete the necklace.

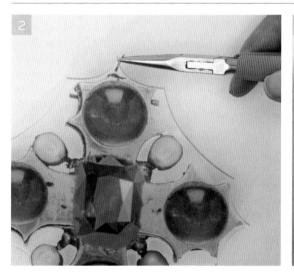

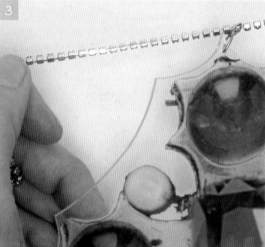

Cut-and-etch motif pendants

For this tutorial, in which you will create pieces for two pendants, you can use the pattern that you will make for your Bangle (pages 94–105). Acrylic is used for this tutorial, but you could also use plywood with a paper-backed veneer in a similar way to the Bangle tutorial.

Step 1

Create a new document with an artboard size of 2000 mm (78.74 in) wide and 2000 mm (78.74 in) high, and name it cut-and-etch_pendants. In Advanced Options change the Colour Mode to RGB and click OK.

File > New

Select the Ellipse tool from the Tools panel and draw an ellipse. In the Control panel, change both the W value and the H value to 65 mm (2.56 in) to create a circle.

In the Tools panel, select Stroke and change the sliders in the Colour panel to magenta (R:255, G:0 and B:255).

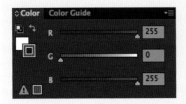

In the Appearance panel, change the stroke weight to 1 pt by clicking on the right-hand side of the bar and typing in the new weight. Select Fill by clicking on the right-hand side of the bar. Click on the down arrow while holding down the Shift key and select a fill of None.

Step 1 (continued)

For the first pendant, select the Selection tool from the Tools panel and, holding down the Alt key, click on the circle and drag to duplicate, placing this circle to the right of the first. Duplicate another circle and place it centrally beneath the first two circles, with a gap between the two rows.

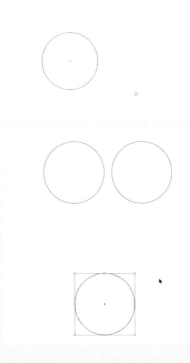

Select > All and duplicate the three circles, placing them to the right.

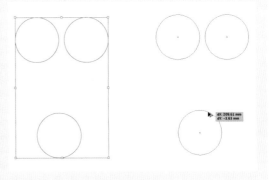

Step 2

Now select the Rectangle tool from the Tools panel and draw a rectangle. In the Control panel, change both the W value and the H value to 65 mm (2.56 in) to create a square.

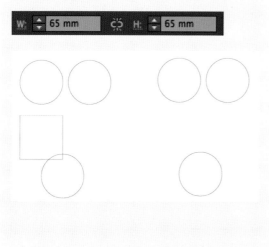

Select the Selection tool from the Tools panel and, holding down the Alt key, click on the square and drag to duplicate. Move both squares so that they intersect the lower circle and are positioned centrally.

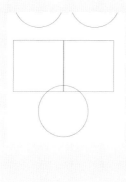

Move the top two circles so that they each intersect the top of the squares.

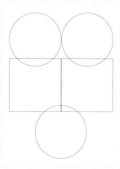

Step 3

To create a set of pieces for a second pendant, start by selecting the Selection tool from the Tools panel and, holding down the Alt key, click on one of the circles and drag to duplicate it. Move this circle to the right of the intersecting squares and circles. Duplicate another two circles and place the three circles in a row.

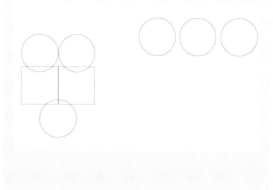

Again, select the Selection tool from the Tools panel and, holding down the Alt key, click on one of the squares and drag to duplicate it. Place it beneath the row of circles. Duplicate two more rectangles and place one next to the first square and the other directly beneath the second square.

You now have the main components of your pendant.

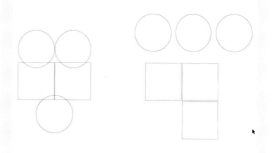

Step 4

Now, on the first intersecting pattern of circles and squares, create the holes through which you will join the pieces together.
Select the Rounded Rectangle tool from the Tools panel. In the Tools panel, select Stroke and change the sliders to green in the Colour panel (R:0, G:255 and B:0).

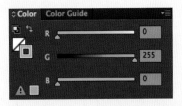

In the Appearance panel, select a stroke weight of 1 pt and a fill of None (see Step 1).

Draw a rounded rectangle and, in the Control panel, change both the W value and the H value to 3 mm (0.12 in) to make a circle. Place it in the intersection between the upper left-hand square and circle to join the two elements.

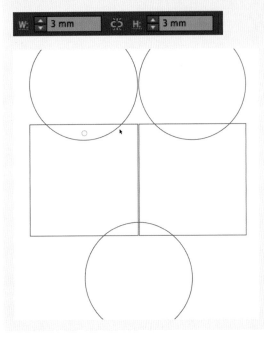

Step 4 (continued)

Select the Selection tool from the Tools panel and, holding down the Alt key, click on the rounded rectangle and drag to duplicate it. Position it in the intersection between the upper right-hand square and circle.

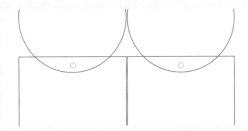

Duplicate both rounded rectangles and place beneath the first two on the squares to join them together.

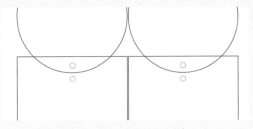

Duplicate another two rounded rectangles and add either side of the join between the two squares.

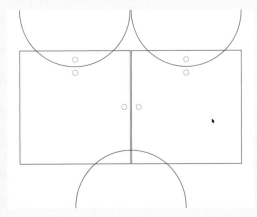

Step 4 (continued)

Add further rounded rectangles on the squares on either side of the join above the lower circle.

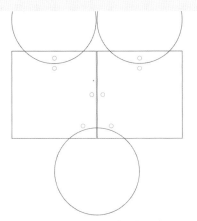

Finally, add a further two rounded rectangles in the intersections between the lower circle and the two squares.

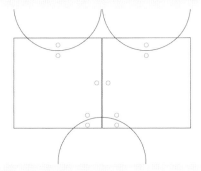

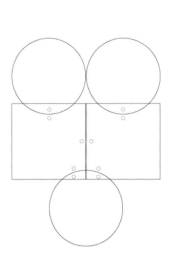

Step 5

Now work on the second set of circles and squares. Duplicate two rounded rectangles and place them on the bottom left-hand corner of the first square and the bottom left-hand corner of the third.

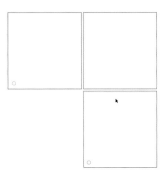

Add two rounded rectangles on either side at the centre of the join between the first and second squares. Repeat at the join between the second and third squares.

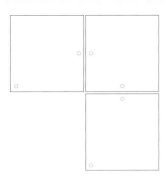

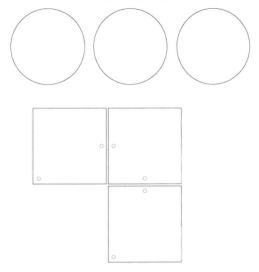

Step 6

Go back to the first drawing. Select the intersecting circles and squares using the Selection tool and, holding down the Alt key, click and drag to create a second set beneath the first.

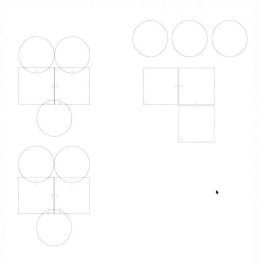

Holding down the Shift key, click on each magenta square and circle in turn in the second set of circles and squares with the Selection tool.

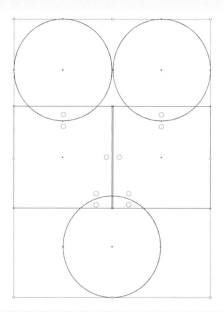

Step 6 (continued)

Choose **Window > Pathfinder** and then select Divide from Pathfinders.

Select the path around one of the magenta squares and circles and double-click to isolate. (Layer 1 <Group> will appear in the top left of the screen.)

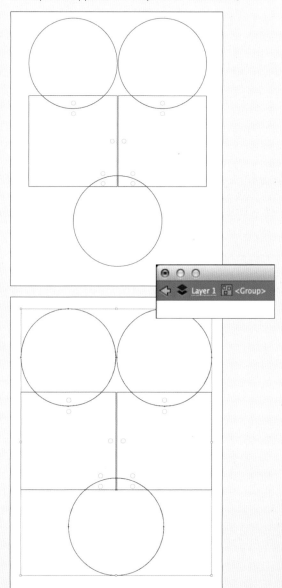

Step 6 (continued)

Select the circles and interior semicircles in turn.
After each selection, delete using **Edit > Cut** until
you are left with two squares with concave curves
cut out of their sides. Add further rounded
rectangles on the squares on either side of the join
above the lower circle.

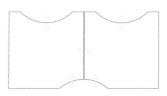

Click the arrow at the top left of the screen
(Back one layer) and then click the arrow again to Exit
Isolation Mode.

Step 6 (continued)

Now select the two upper squares and delete.
Edit > Cut
Finally, delete all the rounded rectangles outside
the remaining squares and rectangles.

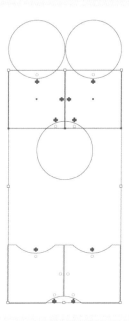

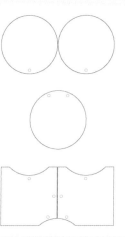

Step 7

Next, place your etch design into your shapes. Open the Swatches panel, Window > Swatches. Click the panel menu icon at the top right-hand corner and select Open Swatch Library and then Other Library ...

Select pattern_1.ai from among the files created for the Polygon bangle (see pages 94–105), or use your own etch pattern. (The file pattern_1.ai is also supplied on the website.) See the Vest tutorial on pages 14–23 for the method of creating your own design swatch.

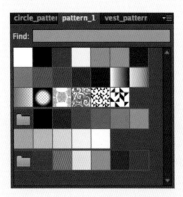

With the Selection tool, select the two left-hand circles on the second drawing.

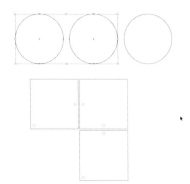

In the Tools panel, select Stroke. Change the sliders to magenta in the Colour panel (R:255, G:0 and B:255). In the Appearance panel select Fill by clicking on the right-hand side of the bar. Click on the down arrow while holding down the Shift key and select a fill of None.

Step 7 (continued)

Click on New Pattern 2 (your etch pattern) from the Swatches panel to fill the circles.

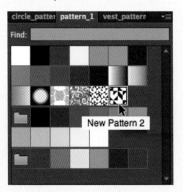

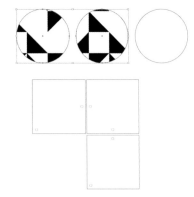

To change the scale of the pattern, hold down the Control key and click the mouse to bring up a menu; select **Transform > Scale**. In the Scale dialogue box, select Uniform and change the scale to 35 per cent. Ensure that only Transform Patterns is ticked and click OK.

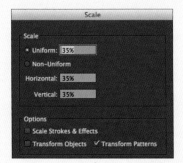

Step 8

Now change the magenta stroke to 0.05 pt for the laser cutter. Highlight one of the magenta circles or squares and choose **Select > Same > Stroke Colour.** Change the stroke weight to 0.05 pt in the Control panel.
Finally, save the file as cut-and-etch_pendants.ai.
File > Save As

Making instructions

Step 1
Cut and engrave your shapes. You can also use the round shapes left over from the centre of your bangle (pages 94–105).

Step 2
To create the first pendant, join the two squares and three circles together with jewellery links.

Step 3
To create the second necklace, join the three squares with jewellery links. Remove the backing from a circle.

Step 4
Apply glue to the back of the engraved circle. Apply to the lower of the three squares. Finish by threading your chosen necklace chain through the rings on the upper two squares.

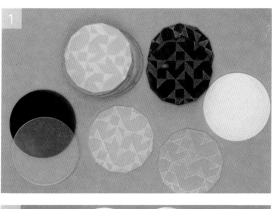

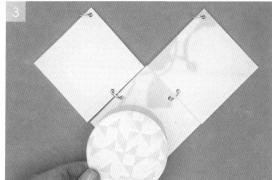

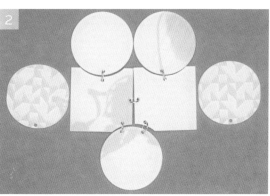

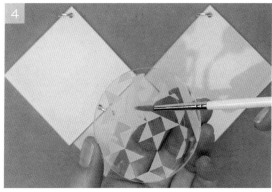

Shawl / diamond pattern

This tutorial shows you how to:

* bond a pattern cut from a solid material such as wood veneer, cork or vinyl on to a textile base to create a three-dimensional finish;

* create a pattern of geometric shapes inspired by tiling.

The pattern for this shawl is created from a simple diamond-shaped motif pattern. You can either make your own or use the shape provided on the website. Cut the pattern from wood veneer, cork, vinyl or even a combination of all three. The all-white shawl shown below left uses laser-cut pieces of the same fabric, bonded on to the base material.

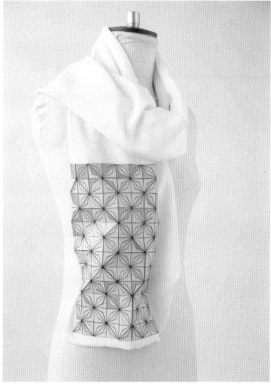

For this project you can use the file provided on the website, veneer_final.ai, and move straight to the making instructions on page 83.

Step 1

Begin by creating the first unit of the motif. Select File > Open to open the template for the veneer motif, veneer_template.ai. This file is provided on the website.

From the Tools panel choose a fill of None and a stroke of black.

Select the diamond shape with the Selection tool.

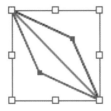

View > Snap to Point
Select the diamond shape and drag it to the top left-hand corner of the document.

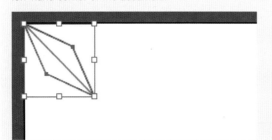

Step 1 (continued)

With the diamond shape still selected, make a duplicate. **Edit > Copy, Edit > Paste**

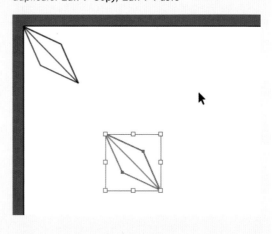

Holding down the Control key, click the mouse to bring up a menu. Choose **Transform > Reflect**, then in the Reflect dialogue box select Horizontal and an angle of 0 degrees. Click Preview and then click OK.

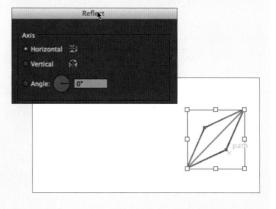

With the Selection tool, drag the second diamond shape beneath the first. You now have the first unit of the motif.

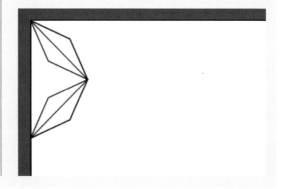

Step 2

To duplicate the unit to a vertical line down the left-hand side of the document, select both shapes.

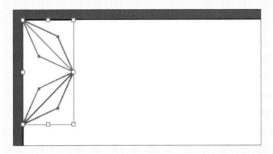

Holding down the Control key, click the mouse to bring up a menu. Choose **Transform > Move**, then in the Move dialogue box enter a horizontal value of 0 mm (0 in), a vertical value of 50.8 mm (2 in) and an angle of –90 degrees. Choose Preview. Click Copy.

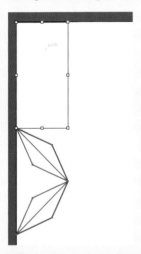

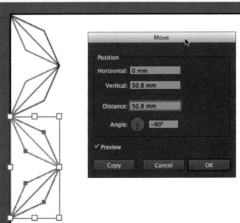

Step 2 (continued)

Press Command+D to duplicate the unit down the page.

Step 3

Now prepare to duplicate the vertical line to create the other half of the motif. In the Tools panel choose a fill of None and a stroke of black.

With the Selection tool click on the upper line of the first diamond shape to select it.

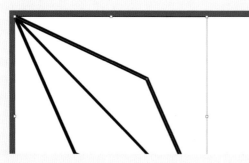

Choose **Select > Same > Stroke Weight** so that all similar lines are selected.

Choose **Object > Path > Join**.

Step 3 (continued)

Now select the central line of the first diamond shape with the Selection tool.

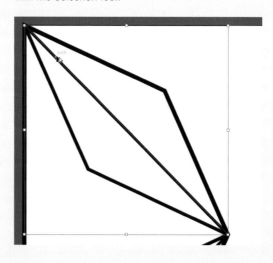

Again, choose **Select > Same > Stroke Weight** so that all similar lines are selected.

Step 3 (continued)

Again, choose **Object > Path > Join**.

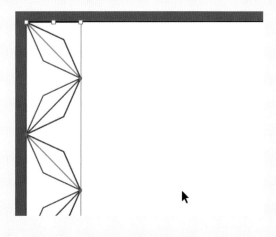

Now select the lower line of the first diamond shape.

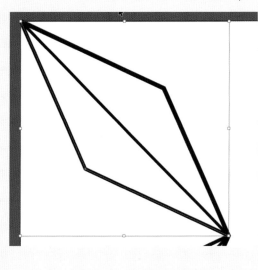

Again, choose **Select > Same > Stroke Weight** so that all similar lines are selected.

Step 3 (continued)

This time, choose **Select > All**.

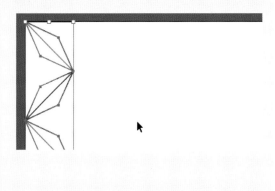

To duplicate the vertical line, select **Edit > Copy** and then **Edit > Paste**.

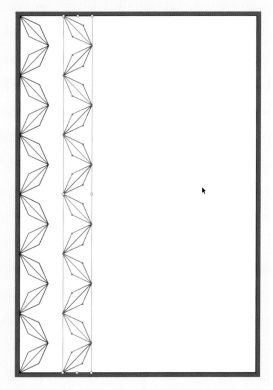

Step 4

Next you need to mirror the first line of the pattern to complete the motifs. With the second line still selected, hold down the Control key and click the mouse to bring up a menu. Choose **Transform > Reflect**. In the Reflect dialogue box select Vertical and an angle of 90 degrees. Choose Preview and click OK.

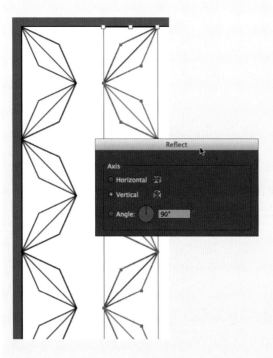

Drag the second line so that it lines up with the first to create the first complete line of motifs.

Step 4 (continued)

Now duplicate the entire line of complete motifs across the page. First **Select > All**.

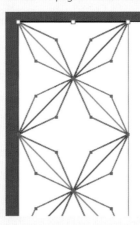

Hold down the Control key and click the mouse to bring up a menu. Choose **Transform > Move**, then in the Move dialogue box enter a horizontal value of 50.8 mm (2 in) and a vertical value of 0 mm (0 in). Choose a distance 50.8 mm (2 in) and an angle of 0 degrees. Click Preview and then Copy.

Press Command+D to duplicate the line of motifs across the document.

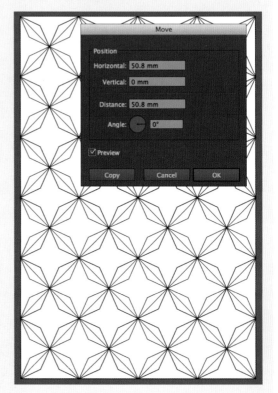

Step 5

Now you need to change the lines to green for an internal cut on the laser-cutting machine.

Select > All, Window > Colour and change the sliders to green (R:0, G:255 and B:0).

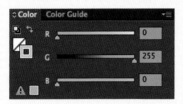

In the Control panel change the stroke weight to 0.05 pt.

Step 6

Now you can add magenta lines, to indicate external cut lines, to the pattern.
In the Tools panel select a fill of None and change the stroke to magenta by adjusting the sliders in the Colour panel (R:255, G:0 and B:255).

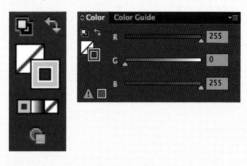

Select the Line Segment tool and draw a vertical magenta line through the centre point of the first row of motifs on the left-hand side of the pattern.

Draw a horizontal line through the centre point of the top row of motifs.

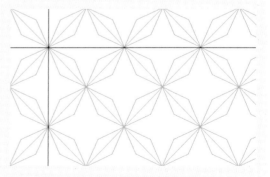

Step 6 (continued)

Checking that you still have a fill of None and a stroke of magenta in the Tools panel, select the vertical line.

To duplicate the line across the pattern hold down the Control key and click the mouse to bring up a menu. Choose **Transform > Move**, then in the Move dialogue box change the horizontal value to 25.4 mm (1 in) and the vertical value to 0 mm (0 in). Choose a distance of 25.4 mm (1 in) and an angle of 0 degrees. Click Preview.

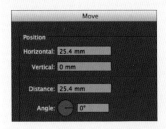

Click Copy.

Step 6 (continued)

Press Command+D to duplicate the vertical line across the pattern.

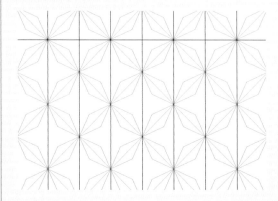

To duplicate the horizontal line down the pattern, first select it and then, holding down the Control key, click the mouse to bring up a menu. Choose **Transform > Move**, then in the Move dialogue box change the horizontal value to 0 mm (0 in) and the vertical value to 25.4 mm (1 in). Choose a distance of 25.4 mm (1 in) and an angle of −90 degrees. Click Preview.

Click Copy.

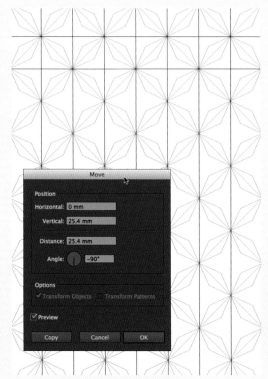

Step 6 (continued)

Press Command+D to duplicate the horizontal line down the pattern.

Finally, save the file as veneer_final.ai. **File > Save As**

Making instructions

Step 1
First cut the file. Now you can use textile glue or Bondaweb to attach your wood veneer or chosen material pieces carefully to your chosen woven fabric in order to finish your shawl.

Step 2
You can cover the shawl entirely with your cut design, or you can experiment by placing elements of the design in sections and combining different materials to create a different overall effect.

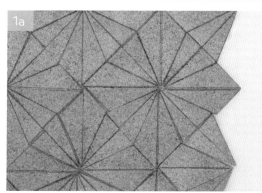

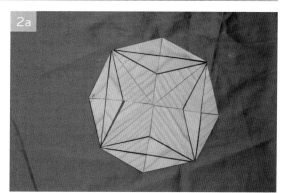

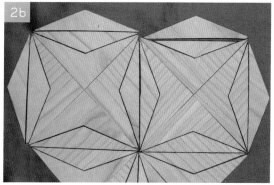

Shopper / monogram motif

This tutorial demonstrates how to:

* align repeated shapes evenly along a path
  using the Blend function in Illustrator;

* make a simple shopper-style bag;

* rescale an existing pattern to tailor it
  to your chosen design.

Here, a monogram motif is created to apply to a
shopper-style bag. The motif can be cut out, etched
or bonded using vinyl-cut self-adhesive foil. You
can use leather, suede, ponyskin or vinyl for the bag.

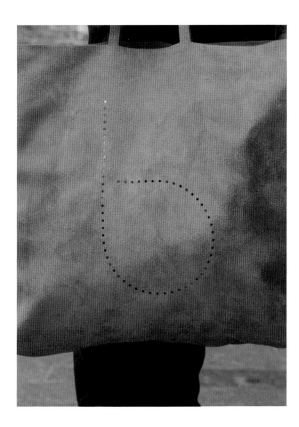

For this project you can use the file, monogrammedshopper.ai, provided on the website and move straight to the cutting and sewing instructions on page 93.

Step 1

Draw your shopper shape or use the template provided on the website (shopper.jpg).
You can use a paper bag opened out as the initial template for the technical drawing. You will then use this drawing as a template layer to make a vector drawing of the final bag shape for laser cutting.

Step 2

Scan and save your drawing in Photoshop, then open it in Illustrator. **File > Open**.
Lock the layer in the Layers panel by clicking in the blank box next to the 'eye' icon.

Step 3

Create a new layer by selecting the icon at the foot of the Layers panel.

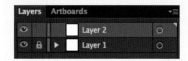

To help you start the drawing, draw a series of horizontal and vertical guides along the lines of your drawing by selecting the Rulers and dragging the guides. **View > Rulers > Show Rulers**

Select the Line Segment tool. Choose **Window > Appearance** to open up the Appearance panel and select a stroke of black and a fill of None.

Now draw the main lines of the bag. With the Line Segment tool first draw six vertical lines. Then draw the main fold lines at the base of the bag.

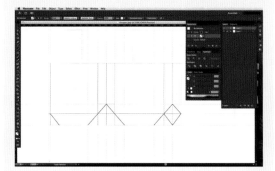

Step 4

Select the vertical line on the far left with the Selection tool. Then choose **Select > Same > Stroke Colour**. This will select all the lines you have drawn.

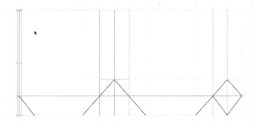

Select **Object > Path > Outline Stroke** to show all the lines you have drawn as dashed. These dashed lines will be etched on to the fabric and can be used as fold or stitch lines.

To change the weight of the stroke select **Window > Stroke** to open the Stroke panel and then extend the menu by clicking twice on the arrow at the top left of the panel. Choose a stroke weight of 0.001 pt. Then click the Dashed Line box and change the size of the dash to 5 pt and the gap to 5 pt.

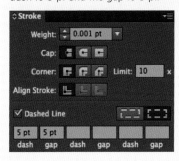

Select **Object > Path > Outline Stroke** to show all the lines you have drawn as dashed. These dashed lines will be etched on to the fabric and can be used as fold or stitch lines.

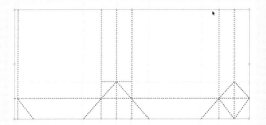

You can switch off Layer 1 to check the result by clicking the eye icon on Layer 1 in the Layers panel, and then clicking again to switch it back on and continue drawing

To draw the handle shape of the bag select the Rectangle tool. Select **Window > Appearance** and make sure that the Stroke panel is open. Draw a rectangle on the inside of the right-hand handle of the shopper.

In the Appearance panel change the stroke to green (R:0, G:255 and B:0) and the fill to None.

Duplicate the rectangle by first selecting it with the Selection tool, then, holding down the mouse, press first the Alt then the Shift key. Now drag it over to the other handle on the left-hand side of the drawing.

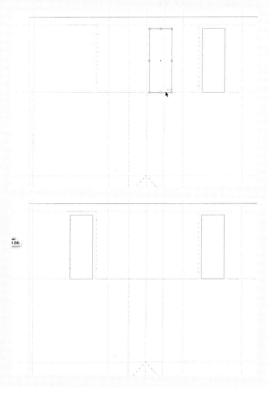

Step 4 (continued)

Select the Rectangle tool and draw a rectangle shape over the whole of the main part of the bag, excluding the handles.

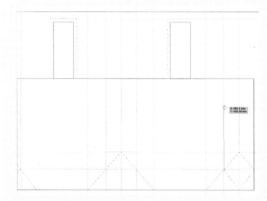

In the Appearance panel select a stroke of red (R:255, G:0 and B:0).
Using the Rectangle tool, draw another rectangle over the outer edge of the right-hand handle and then duplicate it using Alt + Shift before dragging it to the left-hand handle.

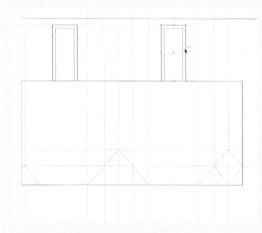

Step 4 (continued)

Now use the Selection tool while holding down the Shift key to select all the red rectangles that you have drawn by clicking on each one. Your drawing will look like this.

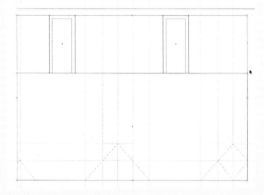

Next select **Window > Pathfinder,** and in the Pathfinder panel, select Unite from Shape Modes.

Select the Line Segment tool and draw a cutaway in the left-hand corner, which will later fit into the right side of the bag when the bag is cut. Change the stroke to red (R:255, G:0 and B:0) in the Appearance panel.

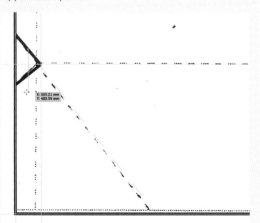

Step 5

Next you will create the monogram design to decorate the bag. Shown here is the letter 'b' used as the motif. Select the Ellipse tool and draw a circle by holding down the Shift key as you draw.

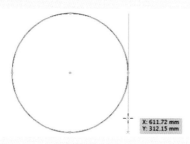

X: 611.72 mm
Y: 312.15 mm

Now select the Line Segment tool. Draw a line and drag it to the left-hand side of the circle to create a letter 'b' shape.

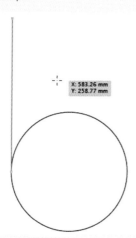

X: 583.26 mm
Y: 258.77 mm

Next draw another line with the Line Segment tool across from the top of the circle, but do not connect the two together.

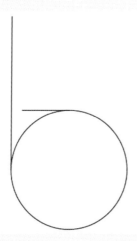

Step 5 (continued)

Using the Direct Selection tool, select the part of the circle between the line that you have just drawn and the stem, and cut it by clicking Command+X.

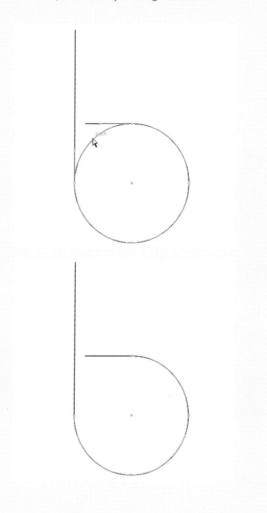

Select all the sections of the 'b' shape (the straight lines and the curve) and press Command+J to create the curve. You will now have a letter 'b' shape.

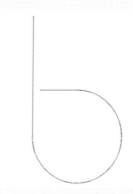

Step 6

To create the cut-out circular line motif for the 'b' shape, first choose the Ellipse tool and, while holding down the Shift key, draw a smaller circle.

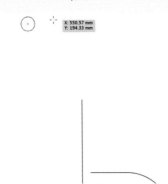

Select the circle with the Selection tool and duplicate by using Alt + Shift and dragging it to the right.

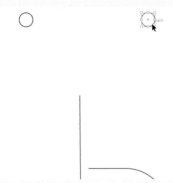

Select the Blend tool to create a line of small circles automatically, which will then be positioned around the 'b' shape. Double click the tool to bring up the Blend Options dialogue box. Choose Specified Steps from the drop-down menu and select 8. Ensure Align to Path is selected in Orientation. Click OK.

Step 6 (continued)

With the Blend tool still selected, click on the centre of the right-hand circle with the mouse. You will see an x next to the Blend tool. Click again with the mouse on the centre of the left-hand circle and you will see a + next to the tool. When you release the mouse you will now have a line of multiple circles.

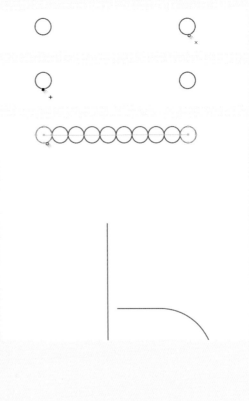

Select the line of circles by holding down the Shift key and dragging around them with the Selection tool.

Then use the Shift key to select the 'b' shape too. You will now see both line and circle shapes selected.

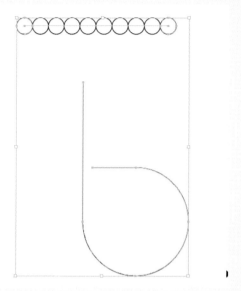

Select **Object > Blend > Replace Spine** to redistribute the circles along the path of the 'b' shape.

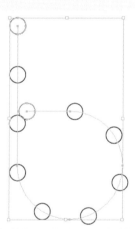

To redistribute the circles more evenly, choose **Object > Blend > Blend Options**. In the dialogue box select Specified Steps from the drop-down menu and then select 20, for example. Click OK.

Step 6 (continued)

Select the Direct Selection tool and, clicking on the centre of the circles, move them individually so that they fit better along the path.

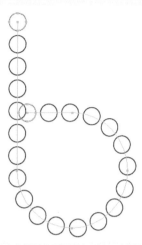

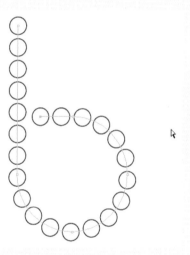

Select the 'b' shape and change the colour to green to signify that the shape is for an internal laser cut. **Window > Colour** (R:0, G:255 and B:0).

Step 7

To place the 'b' shape on the centre of the bag, drag it with the Selection tool to position it, and then Shift + Alt to duplicate it on the other side of the bag.

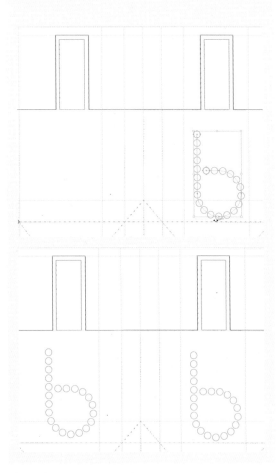

Step 8

Now rescale the document to the size that you would like. Refer to your original technical drawing for scale. Select the Line Segment tool and, in the Appearance panel, select a stroke of black. Draw a straight line with the Line Segment tool. Here, the height is input as 420 mm (16.54 in).

Deselect the guides by pressing Shift and then clicking and dragging around the area outside the bag shape.
Now select the whole bag shape using the Selection tool by clicking on the rectangles. **Object > Group**

Step 8 (continued)

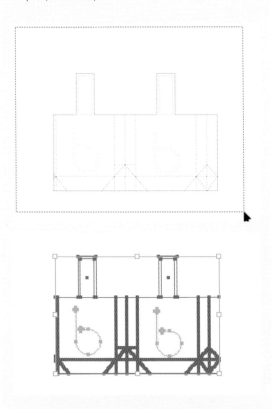

To rescale the whole bag, with the main bag shape minus the handles 420 mm (16.54 in) high, make sure that the whole bag is selected and then select the Shift key and drag the bottom left bounding box handle and rescale against the 420 mm (16.54 in) vertical line. You can use the Measure tool to double-check that you have the correct scale.

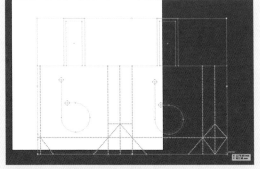

Delete this vertical scale guideline and save the file as monogrammedshopper.ai. **File > Save As**
The shape will now be ready to cut.

Cutting and sewing instructions

You can choose to laser cut the monogram or heat-seal it to the bag using a heat press after you have cut it out.

Once you have cut the shape you will be ready to assemble the bag.

Fold the left-hand edge of the bag over and stitch on to the right-hand edge. Alternatively, you can glue this seam.

Turn the bag inside out and stitch the bottom seam.

Fold the bottom of the bag so that the bottom seam sits on top of the centre fold-line of the gusset. Stitch across the triangular corner.

Turn the bag inside out. Insert a piece of card cut to fit the base of the bag.

You can choose to line the bag with a contrasting fabric. If you wish to do so, you will need to cut a duplicate of the main base of the bag without the handles and motif, and use Bondaweb to attach it to the inside of the bag before you stitch it together.

If you choose a fabric with a blend of at least 50 per cent polyester, such as a faux suede or a polyester-blend suit lining, the laser will bond the edges of the fabric together, so you will not need to worry about any fraying. You can also choose to attach separate handles constructed from 1.5 m (5 ft) of cotton or polyester twill tape, or a 2.5-cm (1-in), or wider, webbing.

Fold down and crease the top edge of the bag to create a 5-cm (2-in) hem. Mark the position of the straps and staple them to one side of the bag. Only staple through the strap and the inside of the hemmed fabric, so that the staples do not show on the front of the bag. Repeat on the other side.

Use two strips of gaffer or duct tape to cover the staples and hem the top of the bag. Trim the extra tape with scissors.

Bangles / geometric motif

In this tutorial you will learn to:

* create a solid object by stacking several identical laser-cut solid shapes together;

* apply a laser-etched pattern on to the surface of your solid object, either directly or with an etched veneer.

This project shows two bangle shapes – one a polygon and one a square. Each is composed of several layers stacked one on top of the other. You can apply a layer of veneer, which you could also laser etch, on the outside surface. You can use either wood or acrylic for this tutorial, or a combination of both, and stack the various shades and colours of your chosen materials together.

Polygon bangle with a square interior

For this project you can use the file provided on the website, bangle_3mm_veneer_pattern.ai, and move straight to the making instructions on page 101.

Step 1

Create a new document with an artboard size of A3 (11.69 x 16.54 in) and name it bangle_3mm_mdf. (This finished file is also available on the website, so you could use this and go straight to step 5.) In Advanced Options change the Colour Mode to RGB and click OK. **File > New**

Select the Polygon tool and draw a polygonal shape. This tutorial uses a hexagon. In the Control panel, click Constrain Width and Height Proportions to lock the scale, and change the H value to 104 mm (4.09 in).

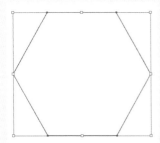

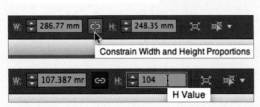

Step 2

To change the outline of the polygon to magenta for an external cut on the laser cutter, open the Appearance panel. **Window > Appearance**

Select Fill by clicking on the right-hand side of the bar. Click the down arrow while holding down the Shift key. Select a fill of None.

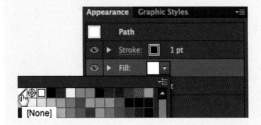

Step 2 (continued)

Select Stroke by clicking on the right-hand side of the bar. Click the down arrow while holding down the Shift key. Adjust the sliders to magenta (R:255, G:0 and B:255).

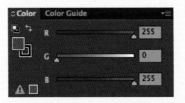

Step 3

Now draw the square for the inside of the bangle. Select the Rectangle tool and, holding down the Shift key, create a square.

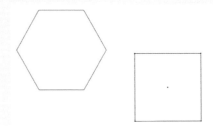

In the Control panel change the H value to 65 mm (2.56 in), ensuring that the 'constrain width and height proportions' option is selected.

Now change the colour of the square to green for an internal cut by opening the Colour panel. **Window > Colour**

Change the sliders to green (R:0, G:255 and B:0). **Select > All**

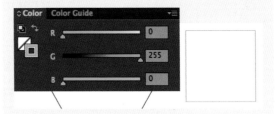

Step 4

To reposition the square exactly in the centre of the polygon to create the complete bangle shape, open the Align panel. **Window > Align**

Select Horizontal Align Centre and Vertical Align Centre.

Select > All
Now duplicate another five shapes. Click the Selection tool. Hold down the Alt key, select the outside of the polygon and then drag the shape.

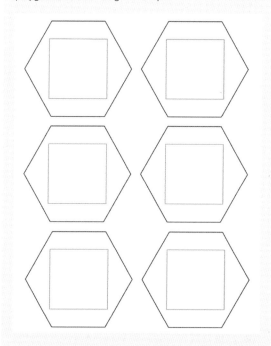

Select > All
Change the stroke to 0.05 pt in the Control panel.

Save the file as bangle_3mm_mdf.ai. **File > Save As**

Step 5

To make a veneer covering, create a new document with an artboard size of A3 (11.69 x 16.54 in) and name it bangle_3mm_veneer. (This finished file is also available on the website, so you could use this and go straight to step 7.) In Advanced Options change the Colour Mode to RGB and click OK. **File > New**

Go back to the bangle_3mm_mdf.ai file, which should still be open. With the Selection tool, select two polygons and their inner squares. Then copy and paste them to your new file. **Edit > Copy**, then **Edit > Paste**

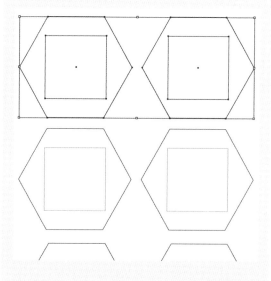

Step 6

Now create the shapes for the veneer, starting with the veneer for the outside of the bangle.

Measure the thickness of your chosen stacking material and multiply it by the number of shapes you will stack. Select the Rectangle tool and draw a horizontal rectangle. Deselect Constrain Width and Height Proportions by clicking on the icon in the Control panel, and then change the W value to 60.044 mm (2.36 in) and, for this example, an H value of 18 mm (0.71 in) – yours may be different depending on the thickness of the material used.

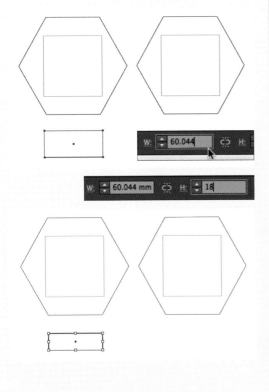

To change the rectangle to green for an internal cut open the Appearance panel. **Window > Appearance**

Select Fill by clicking on the right-hand side of the bar. Click the down arrow while holding down the Shift key. Select a fill of None. Select Stroke by clicking on the right-hand side of the bar. Click the down arrow while holding down the Shift key. Adjust the sliders to green (R:0, G:255 and B:0).

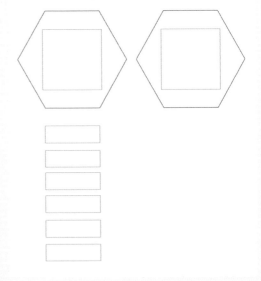

To create the veneer panels for the other five sides of the polygon duplicate another five rectangles. Click the Selection tool. Hold down the Alt key, and select and drag the rectangle.

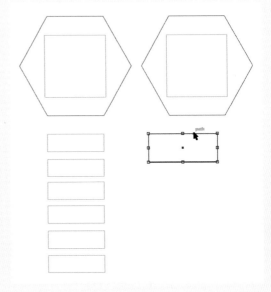

Step 6 (continued)

Now create the four veneer panels for the inside of the bangle. Select the Rectangle tool and draw a rectangle. In the Control panel change the W value to 65 mm (2.56 in) and the H value to 18 mm (0.71 in).

Now duplicate another three rectangles.

Select > All

Change the stroke in the Control panel to 0.05 pt.

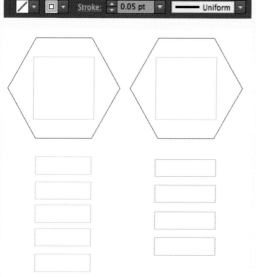

Finally, save the file as bangle_3mm_veneer.ai.
File > Save As

Step 7

You can now create a pattern to etch on the veneer. There is a swatch supplied on the website (pattern_1. ai – used here), or you can create and use your own (see the Vest tutorial, steps 1–4, pages 16–19, for the method).

Open the veneer file you have just created – bangle_3mm_veneer.ai. **File > Open**
Save the file as bangle_3mm_veneer_pattern.ai.
File > Save As

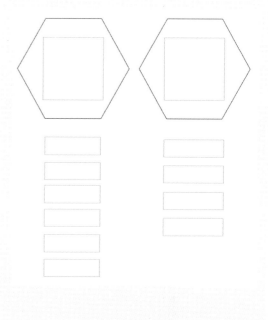

Next open the Swatches panel to find either the pattern supplied on the website or your own.
Window > Swatches

Click the panel menu icon top right and select Open Swatch Library from the menu, and then Other Library ... from the sub-menu. Choose your swatch pattern, or pattern_1.ai supplied on the website.

Step 7 (continued)

Click the Selection tool and select the outer shape of each piece of veneer, using the Shift key to select more than one at a time.

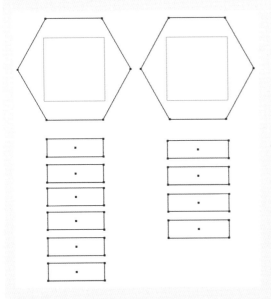

Select Fill from the Tools panel and then select the pattern from the swatch panel you opened earlier.

The pattern will appear in the veneer shapes.

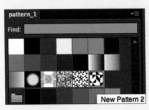

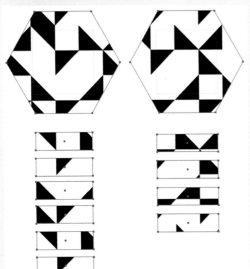

Step 7 (continued)

You can now change the scale of the pattern to fit your veneer shapes.

Hold down the Control key and click the mouse. Select Transform Scale from the menu. In the Scale dialogue box enter the values for the scale you wish to apply. Here, Uniform was set to 30 per cent, Horizontal to 30 per cent and Vertical also to 30 per cent. Click Transform Patterns and ensure that Transform Objects is not checked. You can experiment with a different scale if you prefer

Click OK.

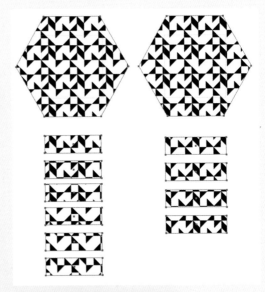

Finally, save the file as bangle_3mm_veneer_pattern.ai. **File > Save As**

Making instructions

When you have finished your shapes you can assemble them with wood glue or acrylic glue, depending on the materials that you have chosen to work with.

Step 1
Glue a stack of shapes together. Glue evenly between the separate pieces.

Step 2
Sandwich the pieces together with some pressure so that they adhere adequately, and then leave them to dry. Here, a stack of five pieces is glued together.

Step 3
Glue a piece of veneer to the top and bottom of the stack.

Step 4
Glue pieces of veneer to each of the six outer edges of the stack and to each of the inside edges.

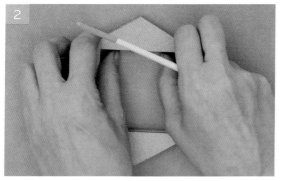

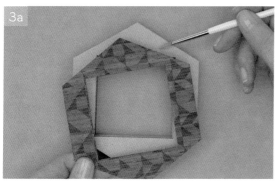

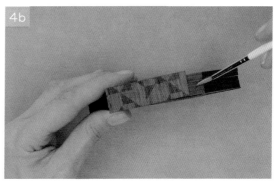

Square bangle with a circular interior

This bangle is made from acrylic and decorated with an etched geometric pattern applied directly to the acrylic. For this project you can use the file provided on the website, bangle_6mm_veneer_pattern.ai, and move straight to the making instructions on page 105.

Step 1

Create a new document with an artboard size of A3 (11.69 x 16.54 in) and name it bangle_6mm_mdf. (This finished file is also available on the website, so you could use this and go straight to step 5.) In Advanced Options change the Colour Mode to RGB and click OK. **File > New**

Select the Rectangle tool and with the Shift key held down to constrain the proportions, draw a square.

In the Control panel change both the W value and H value to 90 mm (3.54 in).

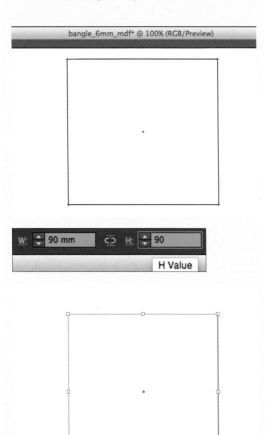

Step 2

To change the square to magenta for an outside cut on the laser cutter open the Appearance panel. **Window > Appearance**

Select Fill by clicking on the right-hand side of the bar. Click the down arrow while holding down the Shift key. Select a fill of None.

Select Stroke by clicking on the right-hand side of the bar. Click the down arrow while holding down the Shift key. Adjust the sliders to magenta (R:255, G:0 and B:255).

Step 3

Now draw the circle for the inside of the bangle. Select the Ellipse tool and holding down the Shift key, draw a circle.

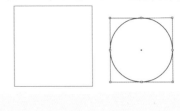

In the Control panel change the W and H values to 65 mm (2.56 in).

Now change the colour of the circle to green for an internal cut by opening the Colour panel. **Window > Colour**. Change the sliders to green (R:0, G:255 and B:0). **Select > All**

Step 4

To reposition the circle exactly in the centre of the square to create the complete bangle shape, open the Align panel. **Window > Align**

Select Horizontal Align Centre and Vertical Align Centre.

Select > All

Now duplicate another five shapes. Click the Selection tool. Hold down the Alt key, select the outside of the square and then drag the shape.

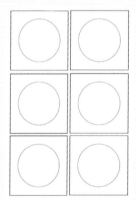

Select > All

Change the stroke to 0.05 pt in the Control panel.

Step 4 (continued)

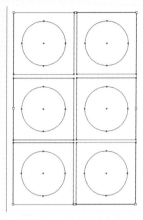

Save the file as bangle_6mm_mdf.ai. **File > Save As**

Step 5

To make a bangle without veneer, you can follow the instructions in Step 7 for the Polygon bangle (pages 99–100) to create the etch pattern to apply directly to the two faces of the acrylic bangle. Then skip steps 6 and 7 below and proceed to the making instructions on page 105.

Alternatively, you could make etched veneer pieces for just the top and bottom surfaces of your stack, leaving the sides uncovered to show the different layers.

Step 6

To make the veneer panels start by creating a new document with an artboard size of A3 (11.69 x 16.54 in) and name it bangle_6mm_veneer. (This finished file is also available on the website, so you could use this and go straight to the end of step 7.) In Advanced Options change the Colour Mode to RGB and click OK. **File > New**

Go back to the bangle_6mm_mdf.ai file, which should still be open. With the Selection tool, select two squares and their inner circles. Then copy and paste them into your new file. **Edit > Copy, Edit > Paste**

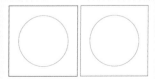

Step 7

Select the Rectangle tool and draw a vertical rectangle. In the Control panel, deselect Constrain Width and Height Proportions; change the W value to 36 mm (1.42 in) and the H value to 204.204 mm (8.04 in).

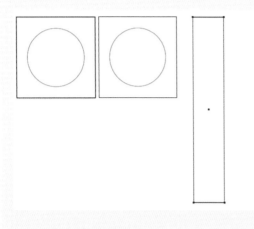

To change the rectangle to green for an internal cut open the Appearance panel. **Window > Appearance** Select Fill by clicking on the right-hand side of the bar. Click the down arrow while holding down the Shift key. Select a fill of None.

Select Stroke by clicking on the right-hand side of the bar. Click the down arrow while holding down the Shift key. Adjust the sliders to green (R:0, G:255 and B:0).

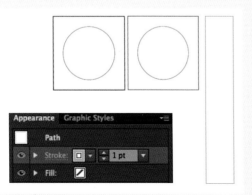

Step 7 (continued)

To create the pattern file for the four sides of the bangle, select the Rectangle tool again and this time draw a horizontal rectangle. In the Control panel change the W value to 90 mm (3.54 in) and the H value to 36 mm (1.42 in).

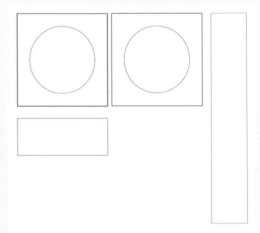

Now duplicate another three rectangles. Click the Selection tool. Hold down the Alt key, select and then drag the rectangle.

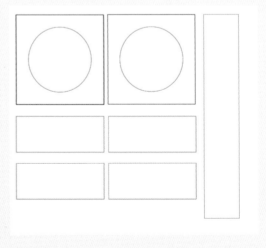

Step 7 (continued)

Select > All

Change the stroke in the Control panel to 0.05 pt.

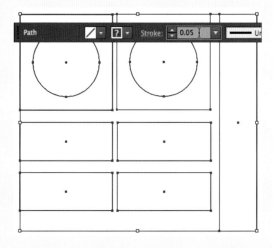

Finally save the file as bangle_6mm_veneer.ai.
File > Save As

You can now create a pattern to etch on the veneer. There is a file supplied on the website (bangle_6mm_ veneer_pattern.ai), or you can create and use your own (see the Vest tutorial, steps 1–4, pages 16–19, for the method).

Making instructions

When you have finished your shapes you can assemble them with wood glue or acrylic glue, depending on the materials that you have chosen to work with. For the bangle shown below, the veneer pieces were not added to the sides; the different colours of acrylic in the stack create a pattern of their own.

Step 1
Glue a stack of shapes together. Glue evenly between the separate pieces.

Step 2
Sandwich them together with some pressure so that they adhere adequately, and then leave them to dry.

Step 3
Here, a stack of seven pieces is glued together.

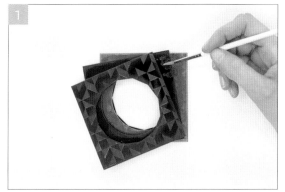

Drawstring trousers / gradated stripes

In this tutorial you will learn how to:

* create a surface pattern file in Illustrator for
  laser-cutting combined with digital printing;

* make a pattern for a simple pair of trousers.

The striped pattern created here uses a colour
gradient taken from a yarn winding. A yarn winding
is made by wrapping coloured yarn around a piece
of card, and is used to produce colour palette, weave
structure, and patterns as part of the woven textile
design process – it is used here as inspiration for a
digitally produced pattern.

You can create a template for your drawstring trousers
by turning a pair of pyjama bottoms inside out and
then folding them in half. A white recycled baby silk
was used for this project, with ribbon for the drawstring.

Step 1

Scan your yarn winding in Photoshop. You can create your own, or use the scan supplied on the website (yarn_winding.jpg).

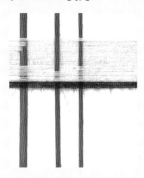

In Illustrator, create a new document with an artboard size of 100 mm (3.94 in) wide and 100 mm (3.94 in) high and name it pattern. In Advanced Options change the Colour Mode to RBG and click OK.
File > New
Place your scanned file in this new file. **File > Place**

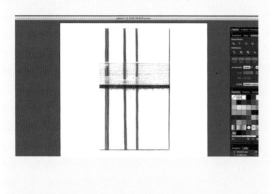

Lock this layer and create a new one.
Window > Layers
Click in the blank box to the right of the 'eye' icon next to Layer 1. Then click Create New Layer at the bottom of the Layers panel. Alternatively, you can click the panel menu icon and select New Layer, then click OK in the Layers Options panel.

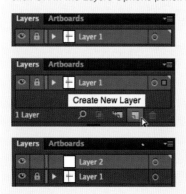

Step 2

Now use the yarn winding as a template to create the shape of your stripes. Start by selecting the Rectangle tool and changing its appearance to white with no outline. **Window > Appearance**
Change the fill to white by clicking the box to the right of Fill and then holding down the arrow with the Shift key and selecting white.

Change the stroke to None by clicking the box to the right of Stroke and then holding down the arrow with the Shift key and selecting None.

Draw three stripes with the rectangle tool using the yarn winding as a template: one longer than the first, and a third longer again and also narrower.

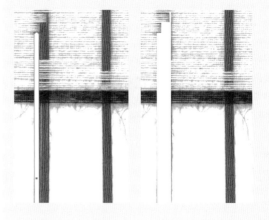

With the Selection tool, select all three rectangles.

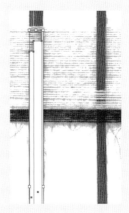

Step 2 (continued)

Now join the rectangles together to create a single stripe. Select **Window > Pathfinder**, then in the Pathfinder panel select Unite from Shape Modes.

To create the gradated colouring in the stripe select **Window > Gradient**. From the Type drop-down menu select Linear.

On the slider, click on the black toggle on the right-hand side. Your stripe should then be gradated to black from left to right.

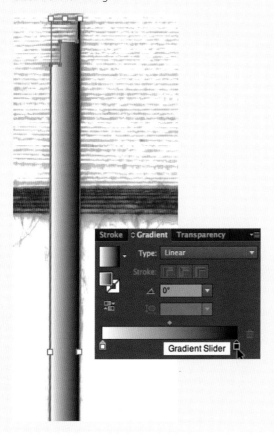

Step 2 (continued)

To change the colours of the gradated stripe, open the Colour panel by selecting **Window > Colour**. Click on the panel menu icon and select RGB.

From the RGB spectrum bar choose orange to create an orange linear gradient on your stripe.

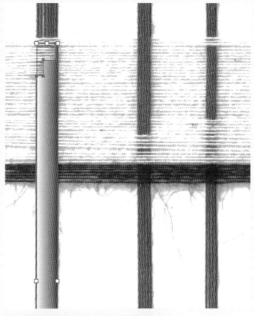

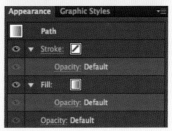

Step 2 (continued)

Now choose the second colour for your stripe by selecting the white toggle on Gradient slider.

Again, click the panel menu icon and select RGB before choosing yellow from the RGB spectrum bar.

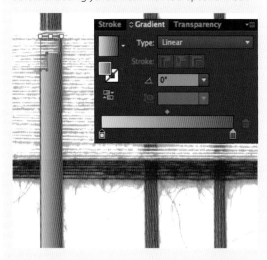

In the Gradient panel, select an angle of 90 degrees from the drop-down menu.

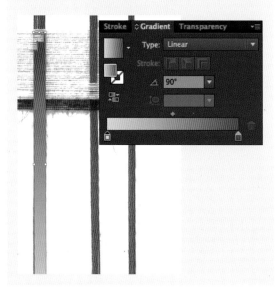

Step 3

Now create the pattern using this coloured stripe. First you will need to duplicate the stripe you have just created to form one long stripe, the stepped appearance at the top of your first stripe becoming part of the new pattern.
With the Selection tool, select the stripe then **Edit > Copy** and **Edit > Paste in Back** to duplicate the stripe, one sitting on top of the other. With the Selection tool, drag the second stripe away from the first, and then position the first stripe on top of the second to create a longer single stripe.

You now need to isolate the middle section of this new stripe to form the basis of the pattern repeat. Ensure you deselect the stripe by clicking outside the stripe before selecting the Line Segment tool. In the Appearance panel select a fill and stroke of None by clicking in the boxes to the right, clicking the down arrows while holding down the Shift key and selecting None.

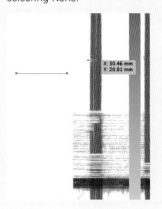

Step 3 (continued)

Draw a short horizontal line centrally across the top half of your stripe. Select the line with the Selection tool and, holding down the Alt key, make another line and drag it down to the bottom half of your stripe, again placing it centrally and horizontally. **Select > All**

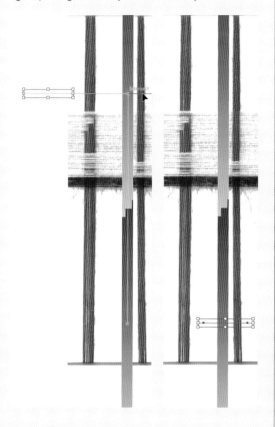

Now you need to remove the top and bottom sections of the original stripe. Select **Window > Pathfinder**, and in the Pathfinders dialogue box select Divide.

Step 3 (continued)

Double-click your shape selection in order to go to Isolation Mode. Select the top part of the stripe and select **Edit > Cut**. Select the bottom part of the stripe and again select **Edit > Cut**. You now have a shorter stripe.

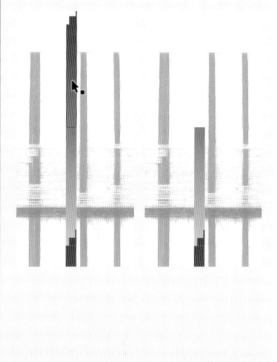

Click the arrow at the top left of the Control panel (Back one level) and then click the arrow again to Exit Isolation Mode. You now have a sample of the repeat pattern.

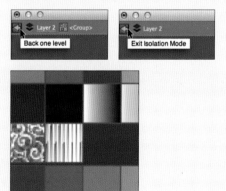

Step 4

To create the repeat pattern, select the shorter stripe with the Selection tool. Select **Object > Pattern > Make**. Click OK to save a copy to your swatches panel.

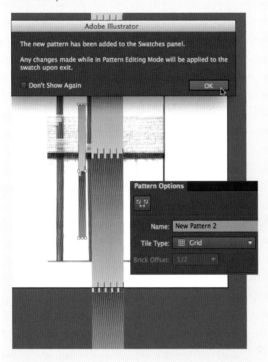

From the Tile Type drop-down menu, select Brick by Column. Change the width to 6 mm (0.24 in). (You may need to adjust this according to the size of your own stripe.) Name it New Pattern 2 and select Done from the Control panel.

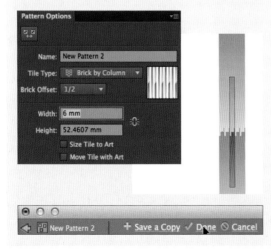

Step 4 (continued)

You will now have a new pattern in your swatches palette. Select this pattern.

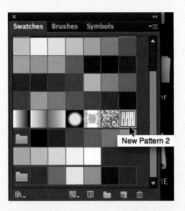

Select the panel menu icon, choose Save Swatch as AI ... and save the file as pattern_swatches.ai. Then save your document as pattern.ai. **File > Save As**

Step 5

With the pattern created, you now need to place it into your trouser pattern template to create a file for digitally printing the fabric.
Open the pattern template for your trousers, or you can use the template supplied on the website to accompany this book – template.ai. **File > Open**

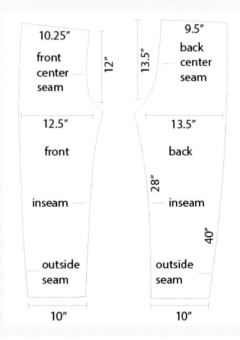

Step 5 (continued)

In the Swatches panel, click the panel menu icon and select Open Swatch Library and then Other Library ... from the sub-menu. Select pattern_swatches.ai. Your saved stripe swatch will open.

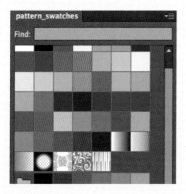

Using the Selection tool select the right-hand trouser leg template. Select the striped pattern from the Pattern Swatches panel; it will appear as the fill in the right trouser-leg template. In the Appearance panel, also select a stroke of black for the outline of the trouser.

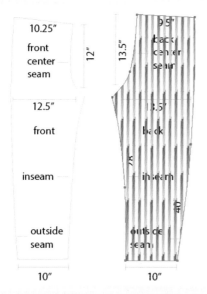

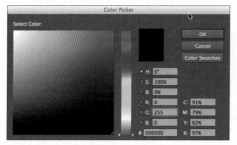

Step 5 (continued)

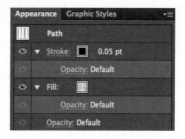

To change the scale of the pattern, press the Control key and click the mouse to bring up the menu. Select **Transform > Scale**. Uncheck Transform Objects and check Transform Patterns. Change the Uniform Scale to 500 per cent and click OK.

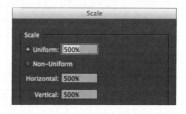

Repeat for the left trouser-leg.

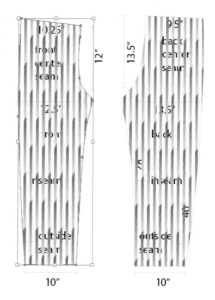

Step 5 (continued)

To complete the file for the digital printer, add cross hairs at the foot of the trouser template to enable the printer to line up the pattern.
Select **Window > Layers** and switch off Layer 1 to hide the template layer by clicking the eye icon next to Layer 1.

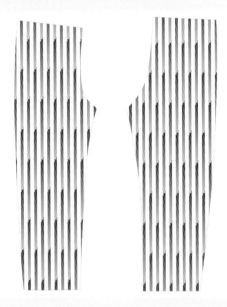

Select the Line Segment tool and draw the cross hairs at the bottom left of the template. Select them with the Selection tool and, holding down the Alt key, duplicate them on the other side of the template.

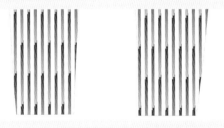

The pattern can be digitally printed directly on to the material, or it can be printed on to heat-transfer paper and applied to the fabric in a heat press. Ensure alignment is accurate at each stage.

Step 5 (continued)

Save the file as a JPEG for heat-transfer digital printing by selecting **File > Export**. Name the file heat_transfer_printing. Select JPEG from the Format drop-down menu and click Export. In the JPEG Options dialogue box, select a Colour Model of RGB, a quality of Maximum and a resolution of High (300 ppi) and click OK.

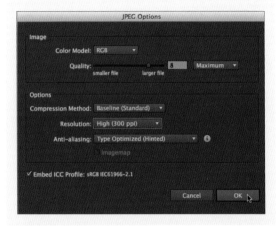

Step 6

In this next stage, you will create the pattern for the laser-cut motif to apply to the fabric. In this design the laser-cut pattern follows the stripes of your digital print.
Start by creating guidelines as placeholders for the laser-cut design element. Select **View > Rulers > Show Rulers** and drag guides from the left-hand side of your screen and place them down the centre of each stripe on your pattern. Work across both trouser legs and place stripe guides over both pattern pieces.

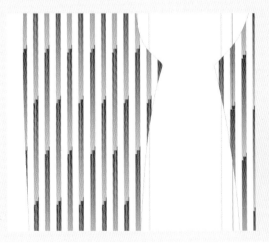

Step 6 (continued)

Place a horizontal guide at the top of the document above the trouser pieces.

Select the Ellipse tool and, holding down the Shift key, draw a circle over the horizontal guide that you have made.

In the Tools panel click Stroke and select green (R:0, G:255 and B:0) in the Colour panel. Change the stroke weight to 0.05 pt. Now select Fill in the Tools panel and select a stroke of None.

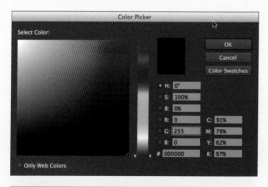

Step 6 (continued)

Select the circle with the Selection tool and copy and paste it; **Edit > Copy** then **Edit > Paste**.

With the Selection tool, move the second circle to the bottom of the template, next to the cross hairs.

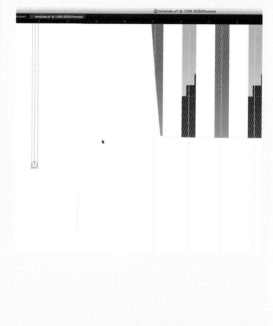

To create a vertical line of evenly spaced circles, first select both circles with the Selection tool.

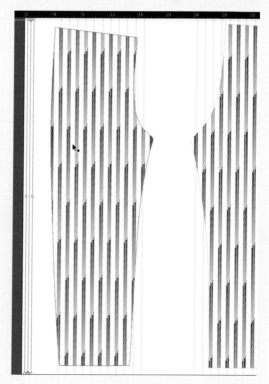

Step 6 (continued)

Double-click the Blend tool to bring up the Blend Options dialogue box. Choose Specified Steps from the Spacing drop-down menu. Change the number of steps to 100 and click OK. (You may need to adjust this number according to the size of your stripes and the size of your circles.)

With the Blend tool still selected, click on the lower circle with the mouse. You will see a + next to the Blend tool. Click again with the mouse. You will then have a line of multiple circles.

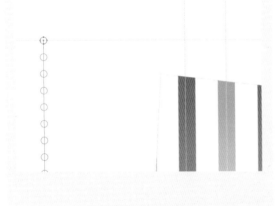

Now select this line of circles with the Selection tool and, holding down the Alt key, duplicate it over your horizontal guidelines to cover the stripes.

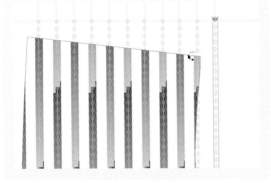

Step 7

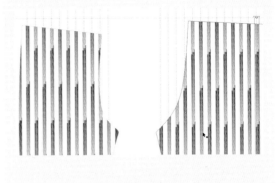

To create the laser-cutting file containing just the outline shape of the trousers and the pattern of circles, select the outside of the left-hand trouser with the Selection tool. In the Appearance panel choose a fill of None and a stroke of black, with a weight of 0.05 pt.

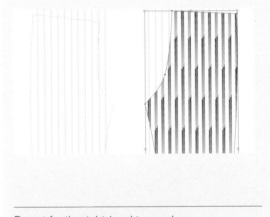

Repeat for the right-hand trouser leg.
Finally, save the file as laser_cutting.ai. **File > Save As**

Printing and sewing instructions

Having printed the fabric (step 5), you will now be able to laser cut the trouser template and ellipse pattern. Mirror your design using the software on the printer for the second side of the trousers.
Then, once the pieces have been printed and laser cut, you will need to stitch the two pieces together.

Step 1

Place the two front trouser pieces together, right sides facing, and pin along the crotch seam. Sew them together with a 1.3 cm (½ in) seam allowance, stopping 6.5 cm (2½ in) from the top. Press open the seam allowance. Repeat with the two back trouser pieces, but sew all the way to the top.

Place the front and back pieces together, right sides facing, and pin and sew the sides together with a 1.3 cm (½ in) seam allowance. Press open the seams.

Pin the front and back inseams together, and sew with a 1.3 cm (½ in) seam allowance. Press open the seam allowance.

Step 2

With the trousers still inside out, create a channel around the waistband for a drawstring. Fold and press the top edge down 1.3 cm (½ in), then fold down a further 2.5 cm (1 in) and press again. Edge-stitch 3 mm (⅛ in) from the lower edge of the double fold, making sure to stitch back and forth several times at the opening.

Step 3

Attach a safety pin to one end of a piece of twill tape or ribbon, and feed the tape through the channel.

Step 4

To hem the trousers, put them on. Mark the hem, then make a mark 2.5 cm (1 in) below this initial mark. Cut away any fabric below the lower mark. Make a double hem. Press, pin and edge-stitch.

The trouser pattern supplied on the website is made to the following measurements:
Inseam: 71 cm (28 in)
Outseam: 101.5 cm (40 in)

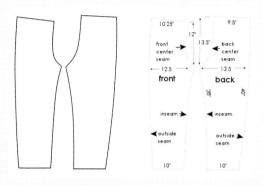

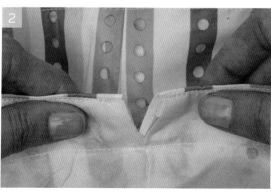

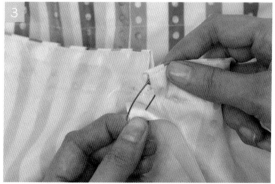

Clutch bag / woven effect

In this tutorial you will learn how to:

* create a trompe-l'oeil woven effect
  using laser etching;

* make a simple clutch bag.

This clutch bag is made with a cut and engraved surface pattern. Ponyskin is used here, but you can use any leather, faux leather or similar stiff material for this project. The variation shown below uses the same Illustrator files produced in this project, but applied to a different substrate – a stiff, hairless leather with shagreen effect.

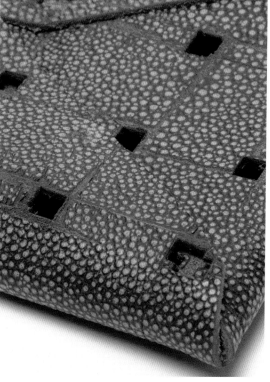

For this project you can use the file provided on the website, envelope_clutch.ai, and move straight to the sewing instructions on page 125.

Step 1

Draw your envelope shape on graph paper (you can open out a paper envelope and use it as a template), or use the template provided on the website (envelope_drawing.ai).

Step 2

Scan and save your drawing in Photoshop, then open it in Illustrator. **File > Open**

Lock this layer by clicking the blank box next to the 'eye' icon in the Layers panel. **Window > Layers**

Step 3

Create a new layer by selecting the icon at the foot of the Layers panel.

Step 3 (continued)

Select the Pen tool, then choose **Windows > Appearance** to open up the Appearance panel. Select a fill of None and a stroke of black.

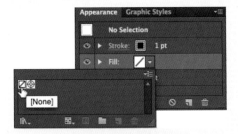

Select **View > Rulers** then **Show > Rulers** and drag a guide to the centre of the envelope. Start tracing one side of the envelope with the Pen tool, using the original drawing as a guide.

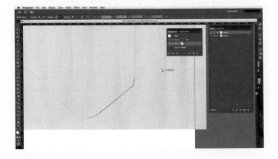

Add another guideline to make sure that the far right flap of the envelope shape is straight.

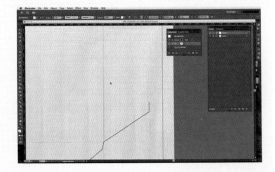

Step 4

Once you have drawn half the shape, you can duplicate it. Using the Selection tool, select the outline path, then hold down the Alt key and drag to create a copy.

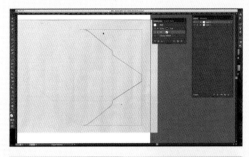

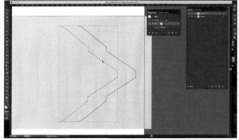

Select Object > Transform > Reflect. In the dialogue box select Vertical and change the angle to 90 degrees. Select Preview to check it and then select OK.

Join the two sides together by dragging with the Selection tool. Select both sides of the envelope by holding down the Shift key and clicking both paths. Unite the two paths to create one object by selecting Window > Pathfinder. In the Pathfinder panel select Unite from Shape Modes.

You now have one object selected. Save as envelope shape.ai. Edit > Save As

Step 5

To create the basketweave pattern, select File > New to open a new file. Specify an artboard size of 900 x 900 mm (35.43 x 35.43 in) and name it wovenbasket. In Advanced Options change the Colour Mode to RGB and click OK.

Select the Rectangle tool. Make a square of W 10 mm (0.39 in) x H 10 mm (0.39 in).

Now draw a rectangle of W 20 mm (0.79 in) x H 40 mm (1.57 in).

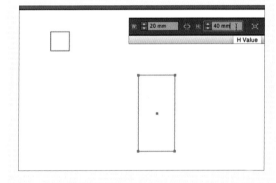

Duplicate this rectangle by holding down the Shift and Alt keys, selecting the rectangle and dragging it to the right.

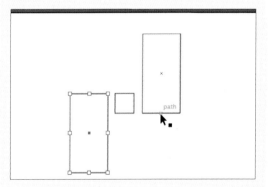

Step 5 (continued)

Duplicate this again and rotate it by selecting **Object > Transform > Rotate** and changing the angle to 90 degrees. Then repeat to create one more rectangle.

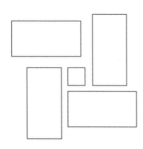

Now move the pieces together to create a woven unit structure (see woven.jpg on the website to check how to put the rectangles together). Lock the layer by clicking the blank box next to the eye icon in the Layers panel – a padlock will appear.

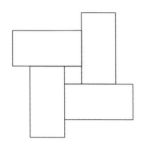

Step 6

Create a new layer. On this layer you will mark those areas of the drawing in red where the lines intersect so that the laser does not cut through the line twice. Select the Line Segment tool to make a line and then change the colour to red. **Window > Appearance**, **Window > Colour** and then move the sliders (R:255, G:0 and B:0).

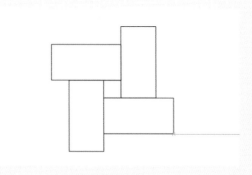

Redraw any intersecting lines in red; the smart guides will help you to position your lines centrally.

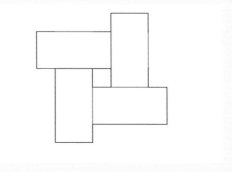

Next select the Rectangle tool and change the colour to green (R:0, G:255 and B:0) in the Colour panel.

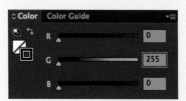

Step 6 (continued)

Redraw the central 10 x 10-mm (0.39 x 0.39-in) square in green and duplicate three more of these squares (by holding down Shift + Alt) and position them on the corners of the bottom-right horizontal rectangle using the Selection tool.

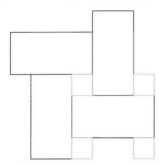

Hide Layer 1 by unchecking the eye icon in the Layers panel.

Step 7

Now you will create the repeat pattern of the basketweave design. The pattern file is on the website (woven_basket.ai) or you can follow this step.

First use the Selection tool to select the path around the drawing and then drag it to the top left-hand corner of the page, then **Select > All**, **Object > Group**.

To begin duplicating the drawing, select **Object > Transform > Move**. In the dialogue box, select Horizontal 60 mm (2.36 in) and Vertical 0 mm (0 in). Select Preview to check it and then click Copy.

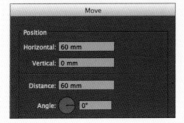

Step 7 (continued)

Click Command+D to duplicate the drawing horizontally across the page.

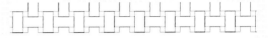

To duplicate this line down the page first **Select > All** and then **Object > Transform > Move**. This time in the dialogue box select Horizontal 0 mm (0 in) and Vertical 60 mm (2.36 in). Again, select Preview to check it, then click Copy.

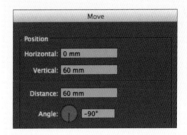

Click Command+D and duplicate the line until you reach the bottom of the page.

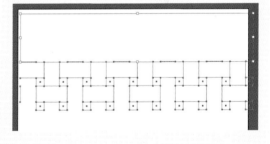

Save this file as woven_basket.ai. **File > Save As**

Step 8

Now create a new document with an artboard size of 900 x 900 mm (35.43 x 35.43 in) and name it envelope_clutch. In Advanced Options change the Colour Mode to RGB and click OK. **File > New**

Copy and paste the Illustrator template you created, envelope shape.ai, into this document. **Edit > Copy, Edit > Paste**

Next open woven_basket.ai and **Select > All** before copying the pattern into your new document. **Edit > Copy, Edit > Paste**. The pattern will cover the whole page.

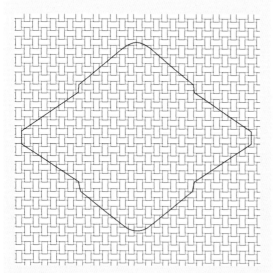

Step 9

Double-click the Eraser tool and change the point size using the slider or by entering a value in the dialogue box and click OK. Select the right-hand bracket key on your keyboard ( ]) to enlarge the eraser and the erase the pattern around the outside of the envelope shape.

Zoom into the edges using the Zoom tool and do not worry about any small sections of pattern overlapping the outside of the shape as you will be cutting the envelope shape out with the laser.

Step 9 (continued)

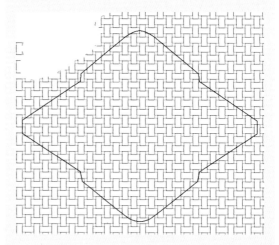

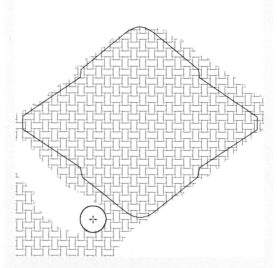

Finally, **Select > All** and make sure that your pattern has a hairline stroke (0.05 pt) in the Appearance panel.

Save the file as envelope_clutch.ai. **File > Save**

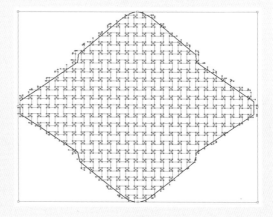

Sewing instructions

Laser cut the woven pattern on the ponyskin first, making sure you leave a 1-cm (³⁄₈-in) allowance around the pattern to allow for laser cutting the actual shape later. When you laser cut the ponyskin, make sure that the grain of the fur is vertical as it will cut better.

Choose a contrasting lining for your clutch with a less heavy or finer material such as a wool delaine. The bag here is made with a fine suede lining. Attach the lining to the inside of the ponyskin before cutting out the clutch bag shape; use Bondaweb or a textile or leather glue, depending on your chosen material. Alternatively, you can stitch the ponyskin to your chosen lining before laser cutting.

Use the envelope file without the woven pattern (envelope shape.ai) to cut out the clutch bag shape.

You will need to use studs and a leather hole puncher to attach the sides of the clutch together.

Step 1
Fold up the bottom flap of the bag.

Step 2
Fold in the right-hand side.

Step 3
Then fold in the left-hand side.

Step 4
Finally, fold down the top flap.

Step 5
With the top flap open, attach one side of the magnetic closure to the right side of the bottom flap.

Step 6
Attach the other side of the magnetic closure to the underside of the top flap.

Step 7
Glue the inside of the bottom flap to the side flaps.

Step 8
Fold the bottom flap back down. On the right side, glue along the lower edge of the left-hand flap and then repeat along the lower edge of the right-hand flap. Stick the bottom flap up on to the left- and right-hand flaps.

For a lighter fabric such as a starched raffia or neoprene, instead of using a magnetic closure, you could just position the studs in Steps 7 and 8 and then tuck the top flap of the bag inside the bottom.

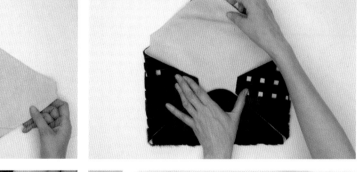

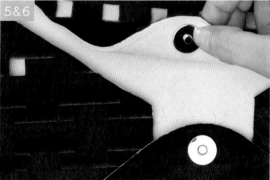

Jumper dress / knitting punch-card pattern

This tutorial demonstrates how to:

* create a surface pattern from a found pattern-
  fragment using the Reflect function in Illustrator;

* make a simple jumper dress or tunic.

This dress is embellished with a pattern motif inspired for a knitting-machine punch card. Find a punch-card pattern to scan, or use the one supplied with the online resources to accompany this book. Once scanned, you can then take a section of the design and redraw it in Illustrator. The dress shown in the main picture was cut into a cotton fabric, and the variation shown below right is laser-etched suede.

Step 1

Open the pattern file for the jumper dress on the website. Select **File > Open** and choose dress_front_and_back.ai. (You can also use your own pattern. The patterns supplied on the website are to scale and were used to draw from in Illustrator.)

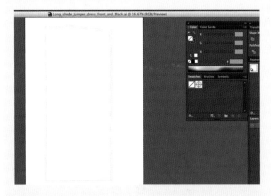

Next, open the scan of the pattern card: jumper.ai.
File > Open

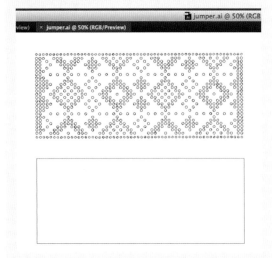

Step 2

Using the Selection tool, select the pattern.

Step 2 (continued)

To copy the punch-card pattern into your jumper dress pattern file select **Edit > Copy**, then select the open dress_front_and_back.ai file.
Go to the Layers panel and lock Layer 1 by clicking in the space to the right of the 'eye' icon.

Create a new layer by clicking the icon at the foot of the Layers panel.

Then paste the punch-card pattern into this layer.
Edit > Paste

Step 3

Now you need to adjust the punch-card motif so that it fits across the width of the jumper pattern. You must first duplicate the motif then mirror it, before selecting areas to join together to create the final motif.

You might find it easier to judge the width of the motif by ensuring that you start with the pattern aligned to the left-hand side of the jumper pattern. Move it by selecting it with the Selection tool and then dragging it to the correct place.

Duplicate the pattern by selecting it with Selection tool, then holding down the Alt key while dragging the copy up and aligning it to the right-hand side of the jumper pattern.

Two files of this motif are available on the website: punch-card_motif.jpg and jumper.ai.

With the copy still selected, press the Control key and click the mouse to bring up a menu. Select **Transform > Reflect.** In the Reflect dialogue box select Vertical and an angle of 90 degrees and click OK. This will ensure that the right-hand side of the final motif mirrors the left.

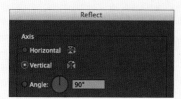

Step 3 (continued)

Double-click on the top pattern.

To join the two patterns, look at the pattern repeat and select a point at which you can easily join the two pieces together. Then remove the area of the pattern that you do not want. If you are using the pattern supplied on the website, select the area indicated here with the Selection tool.

Remove that area by selecting **Edit > Cut.**
Click the arrow at the top right of the screen (Back one level) and then click the arrow again to Exit Isolation Mode.

 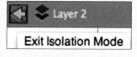

Now double-click on the bottom pattern.

Step 3 (continued)

Again, select the area of the pattern that you do not want.

Edit > Cut
As before, go back one level by clicking the arrow at the top right of the screen, then click the arrow again to Exit Isolation Mode.

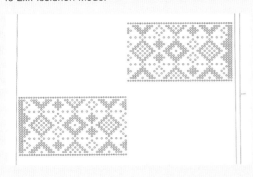

To join the two halves of the motif together, select both patterns with the Selection tool.

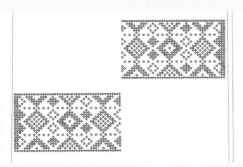

Step 3 (continued)

Select **Window > Align**, and in the dialogue box, select Vertical Align Centre.

The outcome will depend on how successfully you have aligned the two sides of the motif. To adjust them so that they sit correctly together, select the right-hand side of the pattern with the Selection tool and, using the arrow keys on the keyboard, bring it into alignment with the left.

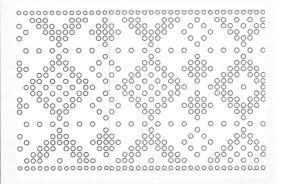

Step 4

Now move the whole pattern into place at the bottom of the jumper pattern by first selecting it with the Selection tool and then dragging.

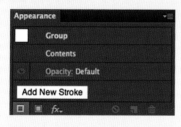

Open the Appearance panel by selecting **Window > Appearance**, then click the icon to Add New Stroke at the bottom left of the panel.

Change the stroke weight to 0.05 pt.
Then choose **Window > Colour** and change the colour to green for an internal cut on the laser-cutting machine (R:0, G: 255 and B:0).

Step 4 (continued)

In the Layers panel unlock Layer 1 by clicking the padlock.

Now change the outline of the jumper pattern to magenta for an external cut on the machine. With the Selection tool, select the outer pattern line.

Select **Window > Colour** and adjust the sliders (R:255, G:0 and B:255).

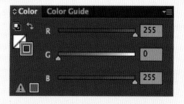

Select **Window > Appearance** and change the stroke weight to 0.05 pt.

Step 5

You now need to select the whole of this pattern, copy and paste to duplicate it, then reflect it to create the front panels of the dress. You will then need to select both sides of the duplicated pattern and copy/paste/reflect to create the back panels. Select the pattern with the Selection tool and then, while holding down the Alt key, drag a copy to the right to duplicate it.

With the left-hand copy selected, hold down the Control key and click the mouse to bring up a menu. Choose **Transform > Reflect**, and in the Reflect dialogue box select Vertical and an angle of 90 degrees.

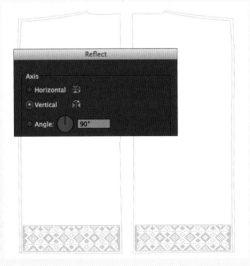

Step 5 (continued)

Now select both pattern pieces with the Selection tool and, while holding down the Alt key, drag them to create a copy.

With the new copies still selected, hold down the Control key and click the mouse to bring up a menu. Choose **Transform > Reflect**, and in the Reflect dialogue box select Horizontal and an angle of 0 degrees.

Step 6

Now add the pattern for the sleeves to the document and create four (two fronts and two backs) to attach to the main pattern, dress_sleeve.ai (this finished file is also available on the website). First open the pattern before copying and pasting it into your jumper pattern file. **File > Open**

With the Selection tool, select the sleeve.

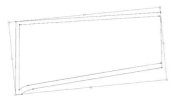

Edit > Copy and **Edit > Paste** the sleeve into your jumper dress document.

Step 6 (continued)

Change the outer line of the sleeve pattern to magenta for an external cut. First select the outer line.

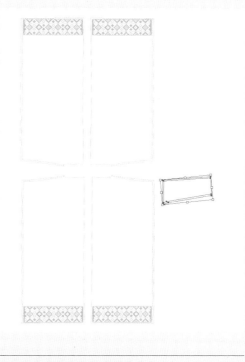

Select **Window > Appearance** and change the stroke weight to 0.05 pt.

Select **Window > Colour** and change the sliders to magenta (R:255, G:0 and B:255).

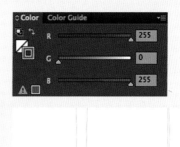

Step 6 (continued)

You can either copy and paste another sleeve **(Edit > Copy, Edit > Paste)** or select the sleeve with the Selection tool and, holding down the Alt key, drag it to create a copy.
Hold down the Control key and click the mouse to bring up a menu. Select **Transform > Reflect**, and in the Reflect dialogue box, select Horizontal and an angle of 0 degrees.

Step 6 (continued)

Select both new sleeves with the Selection tool and, while holding down the Control key, click the mouse to bring up a menu. Choose **Transform > Reflect,** then in the Reflect dialogue box select Vertical and an angle of 90 degrees.
Finally, save the file as dress_front_and_back_final.ai. **File > Save As**

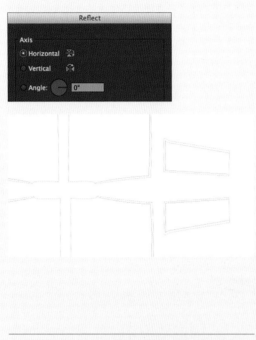

Now duplicate both sides of the sleeve on the other side of the jumper pattern. Select both sleeves with the Selection tool and choose **Edit > Copy, Edit > Paste**. Drag the copies to the other side of the pattern.

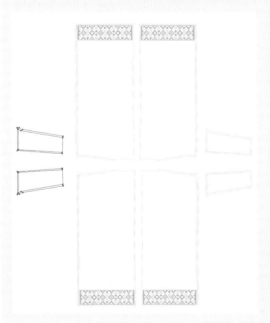

Sewing instructions

Laser cut your pattern pieces.

Step 1
Stitch the shoulder seams together using an overlocker.

Step 2
Stitch the sleeve pieces together along the outside seam. Stitch the sleeves to the front and back pieces, matching the outside seam to the shoulder seam. Press the seams open to spread out the bulk.

Step 3
Stitch the sides and underarm seam in one continuous seam, starting at the hem and finishing at the cuff.

The jumper dress pattern provided on the website is made to the following measurements:
Front and Back (same pattern)
Length: 107.5 cm (42¼ in)
Width: 47cm (18½ in)
Cut 2 on fold

Sleeve
Length: 20.8 cm (8¼ in)
Width: 37 cm (14½ in)
Cut 4 (2 pairs)

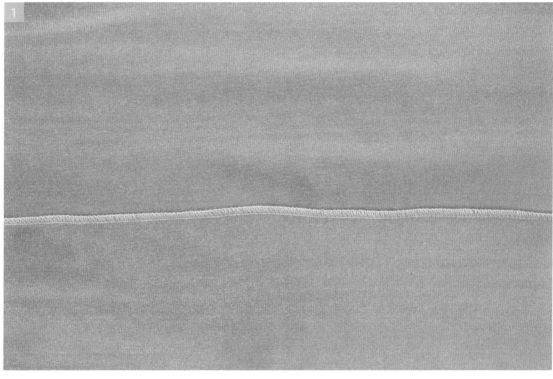

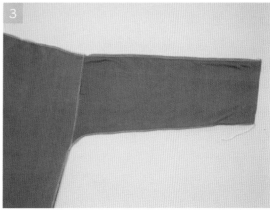

Jacket / honeycomb pattern

This tutorial provides the opportunity to:

* create a regular geometric pattern using the
  Make Pattern function in Illustrator;

* test several fabric samples for different
  laser-etch effects.

A wool flannel fabric is used for this tutorial and
etched with a honeycomb pattern. For a raised
surface pattern you could also use a vinyl-cut flock,
heat-transferred on to your fabric. You would use
exactly the same files to cut the vinyl flock pieces
as you would for etching the design.

If you wish to make a coat, just lengthen the pattern.
The variation shown below right is made from laser-
cut cashmere.

Step 1

Create a new document with an artboard size of A4 (8.27 x 11.69 in), and name it hexagon_swatches. In Advanced Options change the Colour Mode to RGB and click OK. **File > New**

Alternatively, you can use the pattern template provided on the website: hexagon_swatches.ai and move straight to step 3.

First you need to create the hexagonal unit for the pattern with a wide stroke of 10 pt in black.

Select the Polygon tool and draw a hexagonal shape. In the Control panel, change the W value to 103.923 mm (4.09 in) and the H value to 90 mm (3.54 in).

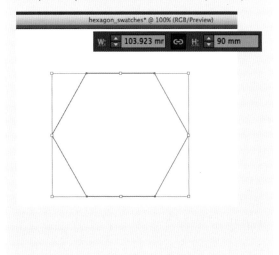

In the Control panel select a stroke of 10 pt. Open the Colour panel by selecting **Window > Colour** and change the sliders to black (R:0, G:0 and B:0).

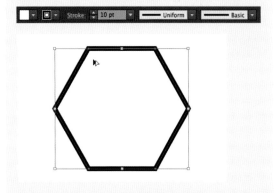

Step 2

Next, create the honeycomb pattern and save it as a swatch to use later to fill your coat pattern shapes.

Using the Selection tool, select the hexagon shape. To create the pattern select **Object > Pattern > Make**. Click OK to add the pattern to the Swatches menu. From the Tile Type drop-down menu, select Hex by Column. Name it New Pattern and select Done from the panel at the top of the screen.

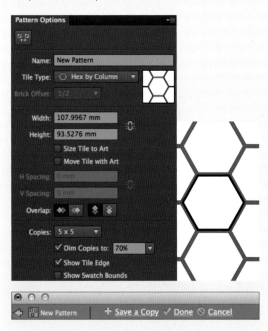

The new pattern is shown in the Swatches panel.

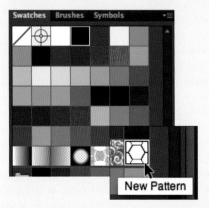

Now save the pattern. In the Swatches panel, click the panel menu icon and select Save Swatch Library as AI ... In the Save Swatches as Library panel save the pattern as hexagon_swatches.ai and click Save.

Step 3

To apply the honeycomb pattern to the pattern pieces of your jacket, open the jacket file and select the pattern pieces to which you wish to apply the pattern. Here, the pattern is applied to each complete pattern piece, including the seam allowances.

Choose **File > Open** and select jacket.ai to use the pattern pieces supplied on the website.

Next, open your pattern swatch by clicking the panel menu icon at the top right of the Swatches panel and selecting Open Swatch Library and then Other Library ... Select hexagon_swatches.ai.

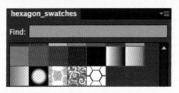

To ensure you fill in the complete pattern piece, including the seam allowances, select one of the outer magenta lines using the Selection tool.

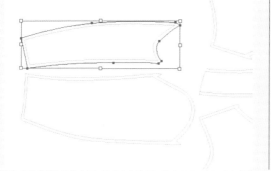

Step 3 (continued)

To then select the outer lines of all the pattern pieces, choose **Select > Same > Stroke Colour**.

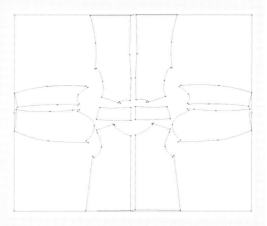

To apply the honeycomb pattern, click Fill in the Tools panel and select New Pattern from the Swatches panel.

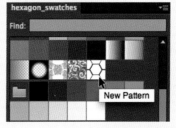

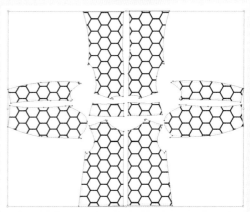

Step 4

You can then transform the scale of the pattern if you wish. Here, the scale is changed to 70 per cent, but you can select any scale you would like.

Hold down the Control key and click the mouse to bring up a menu and select **Transform > Scale**. In the Scale dialogue box, change Uniform to 70 per cent (the Horizontal and Vertical scales will automatically also change to 70 per cent) and check Transform Patterns (ensure Transform Objects remains unchecked). Click OK.

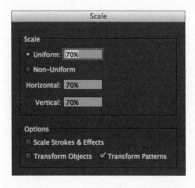

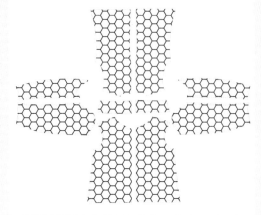

Step 4 (continued)

Having changed the scale, you may now need to reposition the pattern slightly on the jacket pattern pieces to ensure that it is evenly balanced from the left to the right side of the garment, and on the front and back views.

Hold down the Control key and click the mouse to bring up a menu and select **Transform > Move**. In the Move dialogue box, change the Horizontal and Vertical distances (the Distance and Angle will adjust automatically). The numbers will be flexible depending on your own pattern and its scale. Ensure that Transform Patterns remains checked and click OK.

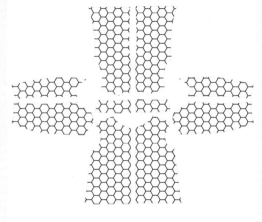

Finally, save the file as jacket_full.ai. **File > Save As**

Sewing instructions

Use the jacket_full.ai file to cut and etch the pattern pieces. Then stitch them together.

Step 1
Stitch the sleeve pieces together along the outside and inside seams. Press the seams open using steam.

Step 2
Stitch the front and back pieces together. Press the seams open using steam.

Step 3
Sew the sleeves into the armholes, keeping the seams open to avoid creating bulk. Press the seams towards the body.

Step 4
Finally, attach the collar.

The jacket pattern provided on the website is made to the following measurements:

Short Jacket

Back
Length: 66.5 cm (26 in)
Width: 32 cm (12½ in)
Cut 2 (1 pair)

Front
Length: 65.5 cm (25¾ in)
Width: 35.8 cm (14 in)
Cut 2 (1 pair)

Collar
Length: 10.3 cm (4 in)
Width: 26.7 cm (10½ in)
Cut 1 on fold

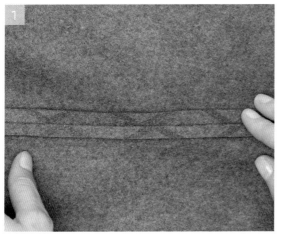

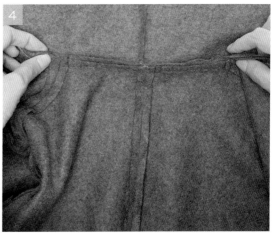

Jumper top / cable-knit pattern

In this tutorial you will:

* create a surface pattern inspired by cable-knit;

* make a cropped jumper.

There are any number of knitted textures that you could use as reference for a laser-etched pattern. Identify the individual elements of the pattern and use the appropriate tools in Illustrator to engineer a comprehensive design. This project uses the Reflect function. A faux suede fabric or a jersey or similar is suitable for this project.

Step 1

Create a new document with an artboard size of A4 (8.27 x 11.69 in), and name it Jumper_pattern. In Advanced Options change the Colour Mode to RGB and click OK. **File > New**

The first step is to draw the cable-knit etch pattern. Start by drawing one element of the pattern and then put it into repeat. To reproduce the lines drawn here and make the pattern repeat correctly, you need to create the pattern carefully within a grid.

View > Snap to Grid

View > Show Grid

Select the Pen tool from the Tools panel. Select a fill of None and a stroke of black from the Tools panel. Then, using the grid, make the first mark with Pen tool.

Click on the next point on the grid, where you want the first section of the curve to end, and, holding down the mouse, drag it to set the slope of the curve, ensuring the direction line ends diagonally two squares away.

Step 1 (continued)

Click on the next square, where you want the second section of the curve to end, and a reverse curve will appear.

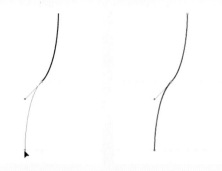

Choose the Selection tool from the Tools panel and in the same panel check that the fill is None and the stroke is black. Select the drawing.

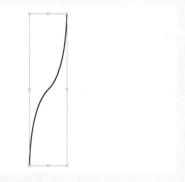

In the Control panel, change the stroke to 20 pt. This represents one side of the cable-knit pattern.

Step 1 (continued)

To create the other side of the cable knit, hold down the Control key and click the mouse to bring up a menu and select **Transform > Reflect**. In the Reflect dialogue box, select Vertical and an angle of 90 degrees. Click Preview and then Copy.

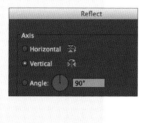 

Click outside the shape to deselect it.

Step 2

Now, using the Selection tool, select one side of the shape to start creating the three-dimensional effect of the cable pattern and copy it. Using the Selection tool, move the copy to the right and place it carefully on the grid as shown. **Edit > Copy, Edit > Paste**

 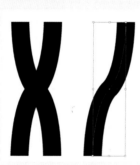

In the Control panel change the stroke to 10 pt.

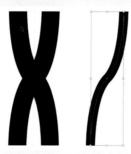

Step 2 (continued)

In the Tools panel select Stroke and change it to white. Double-click the Stroke icon and change the values to R:255, G:255 and B:255.

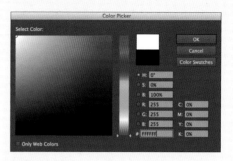

Deselect Snap to Grid by choosing **View > Snap to Grid**. Hold down the Control key and click the mouse to bring up a menu; select **Arrange > Bring to Front**. With the Selection tool, move the white curve across to sit on the left-hand side of the first black curve of the cross. Try to ensure that there are no gaps between the white curve and the black; you can use the arrow keys on the keyboard to make small adjustments.

Duplicate the white curve by selecting its path with the Selection tool, holding down the Alt key and dragging it to create a copy. Move this second curve to sit on the right-hand side of the first black curve.

Step 3

Now you can finish the first element of the cable-knit pattern by creating the straight lines that will run between lines of the cable.

With the Line Segment tool, draw a straight line to the left of the cable pattern, making it the same height as the cross motif.

In the Control panel, change the stroke to 20 pt.

In the Tools panel double-click the Stroke icon and change to black (R:0, G:0 and B:0).

Step 3 (continued)

To complete the pattern, duplicate one more cross motif and place it to the right of the first motif. Ensure the straight line is not selected and then, with the Selection tool, select each line of the cross motif while holding down the Shift key. Then release the Shift key and, holding down the Alt key, drag the cross to create a copy. This is the first element of the cable-knit pattern.

Step 4

Now you can create the complete, repeated cable pattern from the original element. **Select > All**

Step 4 (continued)

Object > Pattern > Make
In the Pattern Options dialogue box, select Grid from the Tile Type drop-down menu.

Select Done from the panel at the top of the screen.

This is the first version of a cable pattern, which will appear in your swatch library.

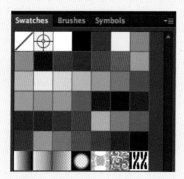

Now you can create the reverse version that will be used for the actual top.

Step 5

To create the reverse version, select the white curves on your cable motif only by holding down the Shift key and clicking on each with the Selection tool.

In the Tools panel, double-click the Stroke icon and change to black (R:0, G: 0 and B:0).

Now select the original black curves and the black line and change them to white. Double-click the Stroke icon and change the values to R: 255, G: 255 and B:255.

Step 5 (continued)

Select > All
Hold down the Control key and click the mouse to bring up a menu and select Group.

Then hold down the Control key and click the mouse to bring up a menu; select **Arrange > Bring to Front**. Next you need to draw a box. Select the Rectangle tool from the Tools menu. Change the fill to white and the stroke to None in the Tools menu. Holding down the Shift key, draw a square box. Change both the W value and the H value to 100 mm (3.94 in) in the Control panel.

Step 5 (continued)

In the Tools panel select a stroke of None and a fill of black (R:0, G:0 and B:0).

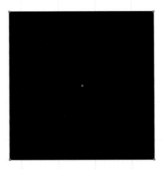

Now select your pattern element again with the Selection tool and move it on to the black square you have just created.

Resize the black square to the size of the pattern element by clicking on the handles at each side of the square and dragging them into place.

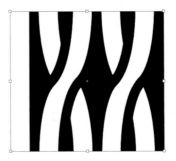

Step 6

Now you can make a repeated pattern from this reverse version of your design. Select the pattern with your Selection tool.
Object > Pattern > Make
In the Pattern Options dialogue box, select Grid from the Tile Type drop-down menu.

Select Done from the panel at the top of the screen.

The pattern is now available in the swatch library.

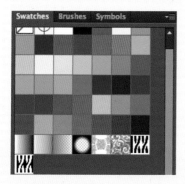

Click the panel menu icon on the Swatches panel and select Save Swatch Library as AI ...
Save the file as jumper_pattern_swatches.ai.
Save the pattern files as jumper_pattern.ai by choosing **File > Save As** and clicking OK.

Step 7

To apply the cable-knit pattern to your jumper pattern you first need to trace the outline of each pattern shape in magenta for an external cut.

Create a new document with an artboard 2000 mm (78.74 in) wide and 2000 mm (78.74 in) high, and name it jumper template. In Advanced Options change the Colour Mode to RGB and click OK.
File > New

Next import the pattern shapes into the file. Here, the shapes were photographed and the photo imported into the new file. You can use the photographs provided on the website (pattern-shape_back.jpg, pattern-shape_front.jpg, pattern-shape_sleeve.jpg) or you can create your own. **File > Place**

In the Layers panel, lock Layer 1 by clicking the blank box next to the eye icon.

Create a new layer, Layer 2, by selecting the icon at the foot of the Layers panel.

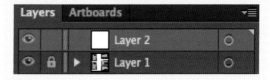

Next select the Pen tool from the Tools panel, and in the Tools panel change the stroke to magenta. Double-click the Stroke icon and change the values to R: 255, G: 0 and B: 255.

In the Appearance panel change the stroke weight to 1 pt to help you see the lines you are drawing clearly. Select a fill of None.

Using the photo as a template, draw around each of the pattern shapes with the Pen tool.

Step 8

The next stage is to scale the templates to the correct size.
Start by turning off Layer 1 by clicking the eye icon in the Layers panel. Create a new layer, Layer 3, by selecting the icon at the foot of the Layers panel.

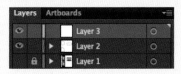

Now select the Rectangle tool from the Tools panel to create a rectangle the exact size of your final pattern piece.
In the Appearance panel select Stroke and change the colour to black by clicking on the down arrow and holding down the Shift key, then changing the sliders (R:0, G:0 and B:0). Select a stroke weight of 1 pt.

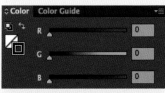

Ensuring you are on Layer 3 in the Layers panel, draw a rectangle and change the W value in the Control panel to 305 mm (12 in) and the H value to 520 mm (20.47 in). This is for the back bodice of the jumper.

Draw another rectangle and change the W value in the Control panel to 501 mm (19.72 in) and the H value to 210 mm (8.27 in). This is for the sleeve.

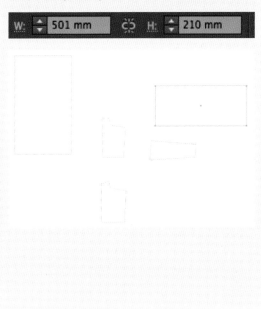

Duplicate the first rectangle, which will be for the front bodice, by selecting it with the Selection tool, holding down the Alt key and dragging it.

Step 8 (continued)

Move the back bodice of the jumper to the first rectangle and then resize it to fit the box by dragging one of the handles at the corner while holding down the Shift key to keep the pattern piece to scale. The centre back and front of the pattern needs to overlap the outside of the box slightly so that the pattern pieces can be joined in Step 11.

Repeat for the front bodice of the jumper, dragging it to and resizing it in the second, duplicated rectangle.

Step 9

Next, you will create the complete pattern pieces for the front and back bodice, as you do not want a seam at the centre front or back. Select both the front and the back bodice pattern pieces with the Selection tool.

Hold down the Control key and click the mouse to bring up a menu and select Reflect. Select Vertical and then click Copy.

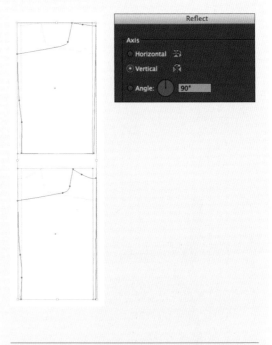

Move the sleeve pattern shape to the horizontal rectangle. Because this shape is not completely horizontal, you will need to rotate it in the box before resizing it. You can do that by clicking outside one of the handles at the corner of the pattern shape and moving it.

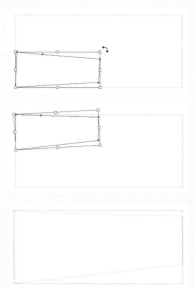

With the Selection tool, click on one of pieces and drag it until it snaps to the other at the centre front and back.

Step 10

Now you need to create a pair of sleeves, each with a front and back pattern piece. Start by selecting the sleeve with the Selection tool.

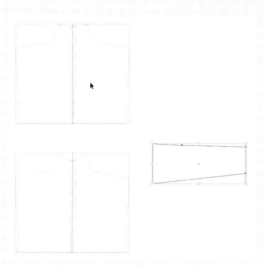

Hold down the Control key and click the mouse to bring up a menu and select Reflect. Select Horizontal and then click Copy.

Again, as you did for the bodice pieces, click and drag them apart, but this time keep them separate. You now have the pattern pieces for the back and front of one sleeve.

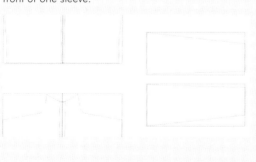

Step 10 (continued)

To create the second sleeve, select both sides of sleeve with the Selection tool.

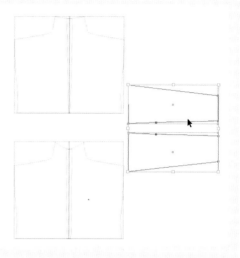

Hold down the Control key and click the mouse to bring up a menu and select Reflect. Select Vertical and then click Copy.

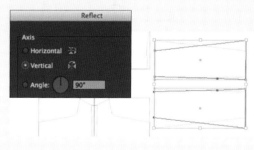

Again, drag the new sleeves to another side of the bodice pattern pieces with the Selection tool.

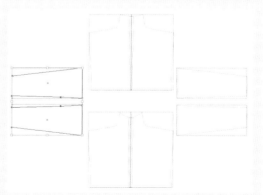

Step 11

Now you need to create one pattern piece for both the front and back bodice.

Start by turning off Layer 3 by clicking the eye icon in the Layers panel.

Select the front and back bodices with the Selection tool.

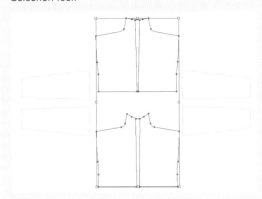

Then choose **Window > Pathfinder**. In the Pathfinder panel select Unite from Shape Modes.

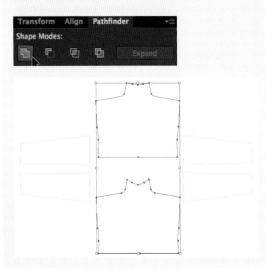

Step 12

Next you can separate the turtle neck and cuffs of your jumper pattern so that they remain unfilled with the cable pattern, imitating a hand- or machine-knitted jumper. **Select > All**

In the Control panel, change the stroke weight to 0.05 pt for the laser-cutting machine.

Select > All again.

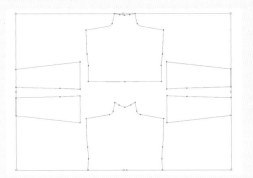

Edit > Copy
Create a new layer, Layer 4, by selecting the icon at the foot of the Layers panel.

Lock Layer 2 by clicking in the box next to the eye icon in the Layers panel, and then turn it off by clicking the eye icon.

Step 12 (continued)

Step 12 (continued)

Edit > Paste to copy your pattern shapes on to Layer 4.

Repeat on the front bodice pattern piece.

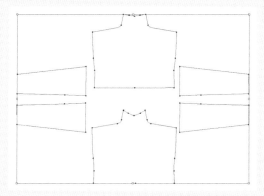

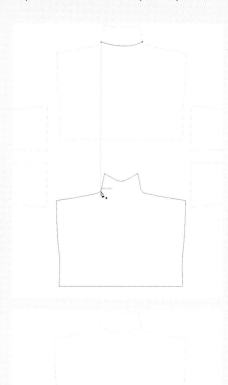

Click outside the selection to deselect it. Starting with the neck, select the Pen tool from the Tools panel and draw a curve around the bottom of the turtleneck on the back bodice pattern piece, making sure your curved line overlaps the edges of the pattern shape on either side. Click on the side of the neck where you wish to start and then click and hold down the mouse on the other side of the neck, dragging it to create the curve.

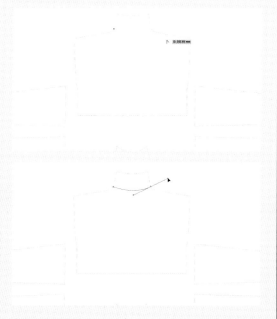

Hold down the Control key and click the mouse to bring up a menu and select Ungroup.

Step 13

Now you can separate the cuffs from the sleeves. Again using the Pen tool, draw a vertical line at the point where the cuffs would begin across both sides of the left-hand sleeve, again ensuring the line overlaps the edges of both sleeves. Click on the first point on the sleeve front and the click again on the sleeve back.

Now you need to divide the cuffs and turtleneck sections from the main body of the jumper and sleeves. **Select > All** then **Window > Pathfinder**. In the Pathfinder panel select Pathfinders and Divide.

Repeat on the right-hand sleeve.

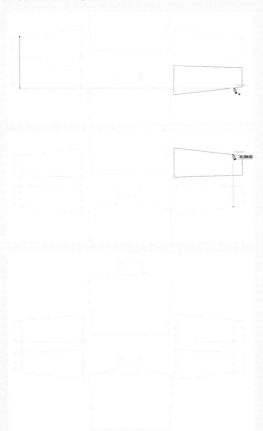

Step 14

Having separated the collar and cuffs, you can now add the cable-knit pattern to the main body of the jumper and sleeves.
First select the main body of the back and front jumper pattern pieces using the Selection tool.

Click the panel menu icon on the Swatches panel, select Open Swatch Library and then Other Library ... and select jumper_pattern_swatches.ai and click Open.
In the Appearance panel select Fill and choose the reverse cable-knit pattern swatch from the Swatches panel.

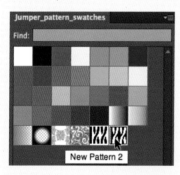

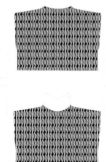

Step 14 (continued)

Next select the main body of the sleeves and then repeat the steps to fill with the cable-knit pattern.

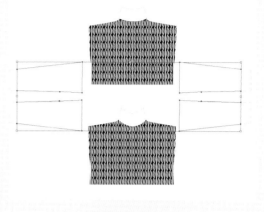

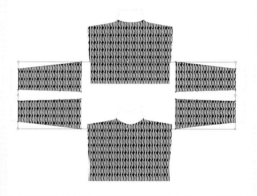

With the sleeves still selected, hold down the Control key and click the mouse to bring up a menu and select Rotate. Select an angle of 90 degrees and check that only Transform Patterns is ticked in Options.

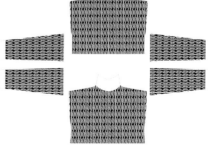

Step 15

Finally, you need to delete the magenta stroke so that just the pattern for the laser etch remains.

Select > All

Delete the magenta stroke in the Appearance panel by first selecting it and then clicking on the trash can at the bottom right of the panel.

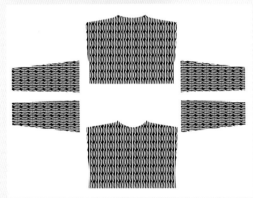

To prepare the file for the laser-cutting machine, choose **Select > All, Object > Group**.

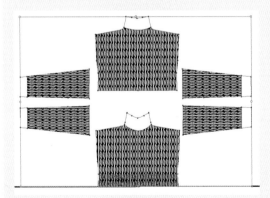

Step 15 (continued)

In the Layers panel make sure that Layer 2 and Layer 4 are visible and the other Layers are switched off.

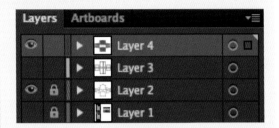

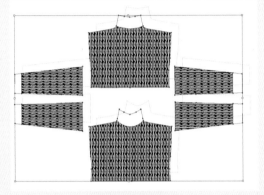

You may need to move the laser etch pattern on top of the magenta outline. In which case, select it and then drag it with the mouse.

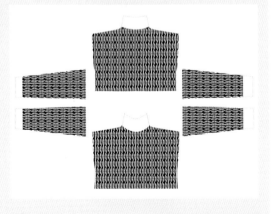

Finally save the file as jumper_template_full.ai. **File > Save As** and click OK.

Sewing instructions

Cut and etch your pattern pieces. Here, the jumper is made from a soft suedette jersey fabric.

Step 1
With the right sides together, overlock both shoulder seams, including the seams at the side of the turtleneck.

Step 2
With right sides together, overlock the two sleeve pieces of the right-hand sleeve along the outside seam.

Step 3
Open out the back and front panels of the jumper and, with right sides together, join the sleeve to the body of the jumper at the armhole, matching the top of the outside seam of the sleeve to end of the shoulder seam. Repeat for the left-hand sleeve.

Step 4
With right sides together, overlock the right-hand side seam of the jumper from the hem up to the underarm point and then continue along the underarm seam of the sleeve to the cuff.

Step 5
The finished, cut, etched and sewn jumper with cable knit-style pattern. By way of variation, you can change the scale of your cable swatch and add details such as ribbing to the neckline, if you wish.

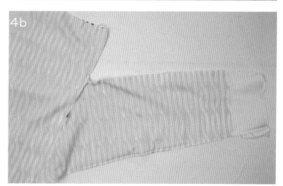

Shift dress / wax print design

This project uses three different techniques to create one garment:

* laser cutting for internal and external cuts;

* applied laser-cut vinyl;

* laser etching.

This surface pattern is inspired by an African wax-print design. In this tutorial you will create a long-sleeved dress with a placement design incorporating varied details – the challenge is to make a design that is unified overall.

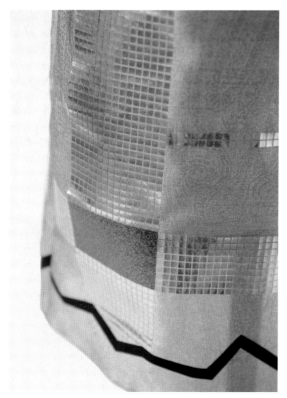
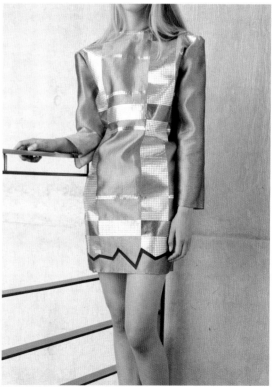

Step 1

The first stage for making the pattern is to create the pattern of five circles, which you will put into a half-drop tile.

Create a new document with an artboard size of 2000 mm (78.74 in) wide and 2000 mm (78.74 in) high, and name it circle_pattern. In Advanced Options change the Colour Mode to RGB and click OK. **File > New**

Select the Ellipse tool from the Tools panel. Select Stroke from the Tools panel and change the RGB sliders in the Colour panel to blue (R:0, G:0 and B:255)

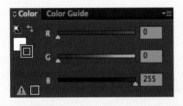

In the Appearance panel, change the stroke weight to 0.05 pt. Select a fill of None, either by selecting Fill from the Tools panel and then clicking on None beneath, or by clicking to the right of Fill in the Appearance panel, holding down the Shift key and selecting None from the swatches.

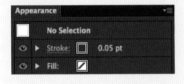

Now, hold down the Shift key and draw a circle. Next, choose the Rectangle tool from the Tools panel and draw a rectangle around the circle, diameter 158.75mm (6.25 in).

Step 1 (continued)

In the Appearance panel, change both the stroke and the fill to None.

Choose **View > Outline** so that you can see the circles to align them in the following steps.

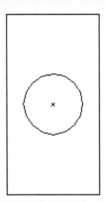

Align the centre of the circle and the centre of the rectangle by choosing **Window > Align**. In the Align Objects panel select Horizontal Align Centre and then Vertical Align Centre.

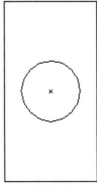

Step 2

Now you need to create the half-repeat tile.
With the Selection tool, click on the circle and,
holding down the Alt key, drag it to one of the four
corners of the rectangle, allowing the centre of
the circle to snap to the corner. Repeat for the other
three corners of the rectangle.

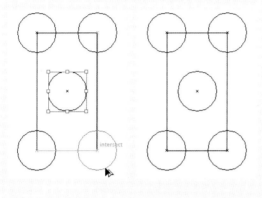

Next, select just the rectangle with the Selection tool.
Hold down the Control key and click the mouse to
bring up a menu and select **Arrange > Send to Back**.
Tick Preview and then click OK.

Finally, **Select > All**. You have made a half-drop circle
repeat tile. Open the Swatches panel by selecting
Window > Swatches and drag your new swatch into
the panel.

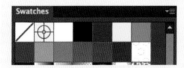

Click the panel menu icon at the top right of the
Swatches panel; choose Save Swatch Library as
AI ... and save it as circle_patterns_swatches.ai,
then click OK.
Finally, save your circle pattern file as circle_pattern.ai.
File > Save As

Step 3

Next, you need the template for your long-sleeved
dress pattern. You can do this from a photo or from
a scan. Either use the pattern pieces supplied on the
website (dress-shape_back.jpg, dress-shape_front.
jpg, dress-shape_sleeve.jpg) or use your own pattern.

Start by creating a new document with an artboard
size of 2000 mm (78.74 in) wide and 2000 mm
(78.74 in) high, and name it dress_template. In
Advanced Options change the Colour Mode to RGB
and click OK. **File > New**

Next place the front, back and sleeve pattern pieces
into the file. **File > Place**

Open the Layers panel by selecting **Window > Layers**.
Lock Layer 1 by clicking in the box to the right of the
'eye' icon. Create a New Layer by clicking the icon at
the foot of the panel.

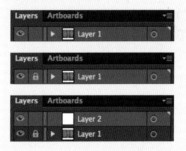

Select the Pen tool from the Tools panel, then choose Stroke from the Tools panel and change the sliders in the Colour panel to magenta (R:255, G:0 and B:255).

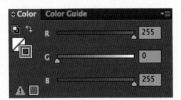

Switch off Layer 1 by clicking the eye icon in the Layers panel.

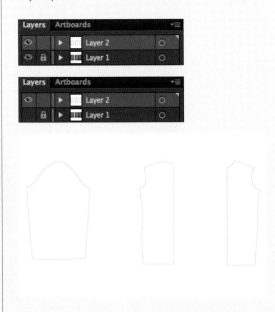

Then change the fill to None in the Tools panel. Now draw around your sleeve pattern with the Pen tool using the photo as a template. Do the same for the front and back patterns.

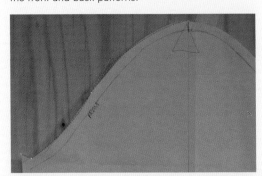

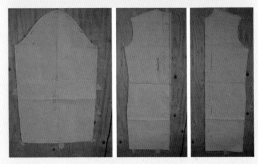

Step 4

To finish the pattern template, you need to ensure the size of each pattern piece reflects the actual measurements of the final garment, and then create the other half of the pattern.
Choose the Selection tool from the Tools panel and select the sleeve. Resize it by changing the W value in the Control panel to 389 mm (15.3 in) and the H value to 629 mm (24.8 in).

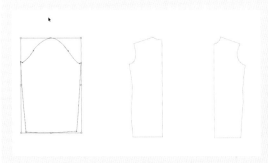

Step 4 (continued)

Next, select the back pattern piece and change the W value to 310 mm (12.2 in) and the H value to 963 mm (38 in).

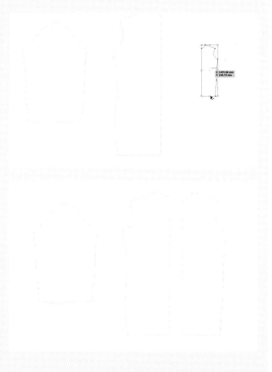

Finally, select the front pattern piece and change the W value to 304 mm (12 in) and the H value to 963 mm (38 in).

Step 5

To duplicate the pieces, first **Select > All**. Then holding down the Control key, click the mouse to bring up a menu and select **Transform > Reflect**. In the Reflect dialogue box, select Vertical and an angle of 90 degrees. Tick Preview and then click Copy.

You may then need to click on the pattern pieces and move them apart. Place the two back pattern pieces next to each other and repeat for the front pattern pieces.

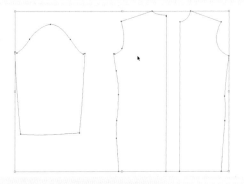

Step 5 (continued)

Move the two back pattern pieces so that they join at the back, and repeat for the two front pattern pieces.

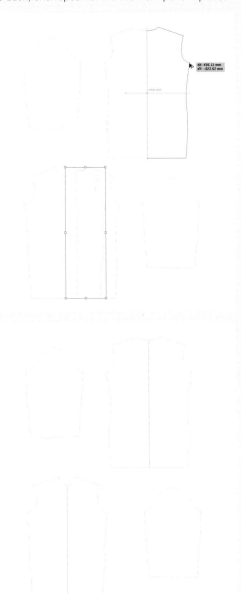

Step 5 (continued)

Select both front pattern pieces and both back pattern pieces with the Selection tool (not the sleeves) and then join them together into one front and one back pattern piece. Choose **Window > Pathfinder** and then in Shape Modes select Unite.

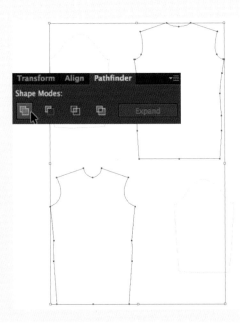

Step 6

Finally, make the stroke very fine for the laser cutter. **Select > All**. Change the stroke to 0.05 pt in the Appearance panel or in the Control panel. Save the file as dress template.ai. **File > Save As**

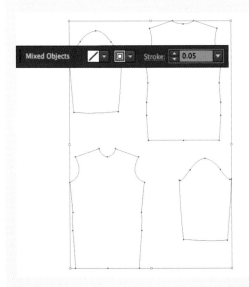

Step 7

Now you can create the stripes for your pattern directly on the front pattern piece. You will find it easier to draw the next stages if you zoom into the front pattern piece first using the Zoom tool from the Tools panel.

Lock Layer 2 in the Layers panel by clicking in the square next to the eye icon.
Create a New Layer, Layer 3, by clicking the icon at the foot of the panel.

Select the Rectangle tool from the Tools panel. Select Stroke, also from the Tools panel, and change the sliders in the Colour panel to green (R:0, G:255, B:0).

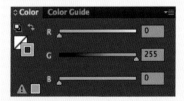

In the Appearance panel, change the stroke weight to 0.05 pt and select a fill of None.

Step 7 (continued)

Draw a rectangle and in the Control panel change the W value to 80.441 mm (3.17 in) and the H value to 42.337 mm (1.67 in).

With the Selection tool, drag the rectangle into position at the top left on your front pattern piece.

Select this first rectangle and, holding down the Alt key, drag it with the Selection tool and position it to the right. Use the guides to align the rectangles horizontally.

Duplicate another rectangle beneath the first one, again using the guidelines to position it directly underneath. Duplicate a third and use the guidelines to position it directly under the second and next to the third. Repeat to create a third row directly beneath the other two.

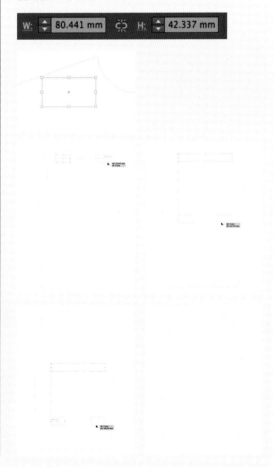

Step 8

Select the Pen tool from the Tools panel and draw a zigzag pattern at the bottom of the dress.

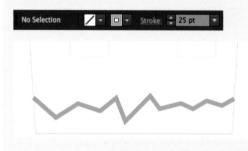

Change the stroke weight to 25 pt in the Appearance or Control panels.

Choose the Selection tool from the Tools panel to select the zigzag and then change it to an outline. **Object > Path > Outline Stroke**.

Step 8 (continued)

In the Tools panel, swap the fill and stroke by clicking the arrows.

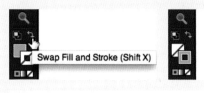

Change the stroke weight to 0.05 pt in the Control panel.

Step 9

Now you will create the striped pattern before adjusting the bottom of the stripes around the zigzag pattern so that they do not overlap.
Create a New Layer 4 by clicking the icon at the foot of the Layers panel.

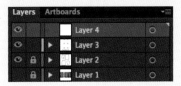

Select the Rectangle tool from the Tools panel. Also in the Tools panel, select Stroke and change the sliders in the Colour panel to blue (R:0, G:0 and B:255).

In the Appearance panel change the stroke weight to 0.05 pt.

Use the Rectangle tool to create horizontal stripes across the green rectangles, extending just over the edge of the pattern. Use the guidelines to ensure that the rectangles are aligned over the green rectangles. Add additional rectangles, making some thick and some thin.

Step 9 (continued)

Create two vertical stripes on either side of the collar of the dress, using the guidelines to ensure that they align with the green rectangles. Try to make sure that these do not extend beyond the bottom of the sleeve.

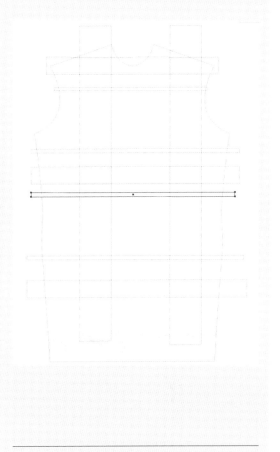

Ensuring that one of the rectangles remains selected, choose **Select > Same > Stroke Colour** to select all the blue rectangles.

Now join the rectangles together. Choose **Window > Pathfinder** and then in Shape Modes select Unite.

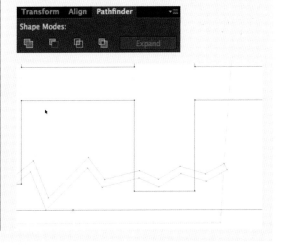

Step 10

Next, ensure that the vertical stripes do not overlap the zigzag pattern, but fit around it instead.
Holding down the Shift key, select both the blue lines and the green zigzag. Choose **Window > Pathfinder** and select Divide from Shape Modes to divide the stripes from the zigzag pattern.

Double-click on any part of the zigzag to isolate the layer. You will see Layer 4 and <Group> in the top left-hand corner of the screen.
Click on the blue triangles outside the zigzag and then use **Edit > Cut** to remove them in turn until you have just a zigzag shape remaining at the bottom of the vertical stripes.

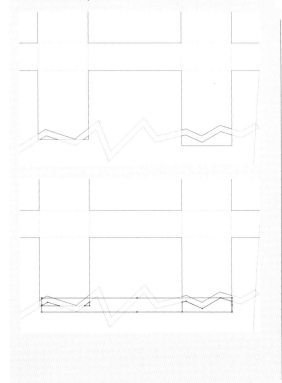

Step 11

Place the circle pattern swatch you created in Steps 1 and 2 into your striped pattern.

Choose **Window > Swatches** and click the panel menu icon at the top right of the Swatches panel. Choose Open Swatch Library and then Other Library ...

Choose circle_pattern_swatches.ai, which you created in Step 2.

In the Tools panel select Fill and then, ensuring the stripes pattern is selected, select the circles pattern swatch from the Swatches panel.

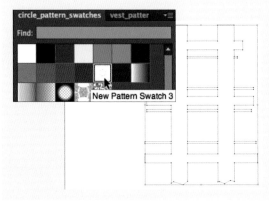

Step 10 (continued)

Finally, reunite the zigzag shape by holding down the Shift key and selecting all the pieces of the zigzag, then choosing **Window > Pathfinder** and selecting Unite from Shape Modes.

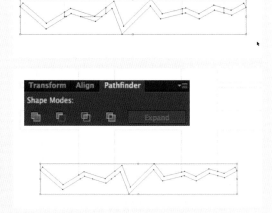

Select Stroke from the Tools panel and change it to None.

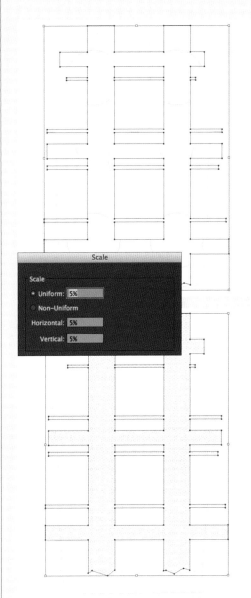

To rescale the circles pattern within your stripes, select the path around the stripes. Then hold down the Control key and click the mouse to bring up a menu and select **Transform > Scale**. In the Scale dialogue box, select Uniform and change the percentage to 5 per cent (the horizontal and vertical scales will change to 5 per cent automatically. Uncheck Scale Strokes & Effects and Transform Objects, and check Transform Patterns. Tick Preview.

Finally, click the back arrow at the top left of the screen (Back one level) and click it again to Exit Isolation Mode.

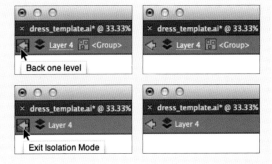

Step 12

Now copy and place the pattern on the back pattern piece. Select > All and then, using the Selection tool and holding down the Alt key, drag the pattern to the back pattern piece.

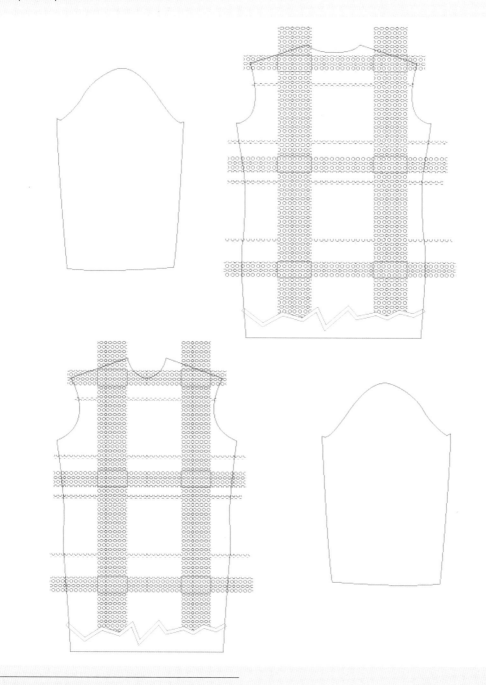

Save your file as dress_full.ai. **File > Save As**
You are now ready to laser cut the pieces, add any vinyl-cut detailing by heat-transfer and then stitch the pieces together.

Sewing instructions

If you are using a fabric with at least a 50 per cent polyester blend, then to make this dress you will not need to finish your seams as the laser will seal the fabric when it cuts the pattern shape. If not, finish the seams or use an overlocker where necessary.

Step 1
Finish the neckline and the bottom of the dress on both the back and front. Stitch the armhole seams with right sides facing.

Step 2
Make a box pleat in the centre of the sleeve at the armhole. Align the centre of the box pleat with the armhole seam and attach the sleeves to the front and back of the dress.

Step 3
Stitch the underarm seam and side seams together, right sides facing. Stitch the centre back seam up to the zip opening and then insert the zip. Turn in the hem at the neckline and hemline, and finish.

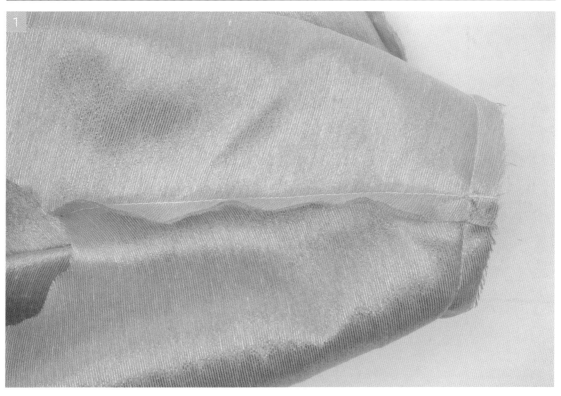

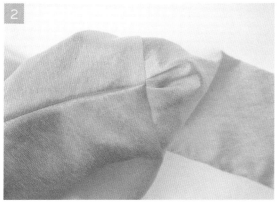

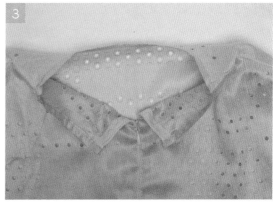

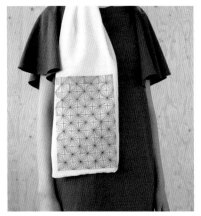

First published in 2016
by Laurence King Publishing Ltd
361–373 City Road
London EC1V 1LR
Tel +44 20 7841 6900
Fax +44 20 7841 6910
E enquiries@laurenceking.com
www.laurenceking.com

Text © 2015 Laura Berens Baker
This book was produced by
Laurence King Publishing Ltd, London

A catalogue record for this book is available
from the British Library.

ISBN 978-1-78067-617-3

Designed by Charlotte Klingholz

Printed in China